to my nephew Dew
Enjoy
Uncle George

The Man From Michigan

By

George E. Davison

Edited By
Robert Curtis

G E Davison

Copyright, 2007
Chandler, Arizona

The Man From Michigan
All Rights Reserved © 2007 by George E. Davison

No part of this book may be reproduced or transmitted in any form or by any means, graphic, electronic, or mechanical, including photocopying, recording, taping, or by any information storage retrieval system, without the written permission of the publisher.

Dominicus Books

For information address:

Dominicus Books
c/o Robert Curtis
P.O. Box 6331
Chandler, Arizona 85248

Printed in the United States of America
by www.lulu.com

Table of Contents

FOREWORD 4

CHAPTER ONE 6
Oscar Davison Family

CHAPTER TWO 23
Growing up in Michigan – The Teen Years

CHAPTER THREE 64
Deer Hunting in Michigan

CHAPTER FOUR 79
The Navy Years

CHAPTER FIVE 107
The Married Years

CHAPTER SIX 146
Deer Hunting, Arizona Style

EPILOGUE 183

Foreword

I would like to thank my sister Donna who inspired me to write this by asking if I remembered the different places that we lived when we were growing up around Fountain, Michigan.

I had no idea what I would come up with when I started this and I hope you don't find this too boring.

You know what they say about getting old: you can't remember what you had for breakfast, oatmeal I think, but you can remember details about something that happened when you were a kid over fifty years ago.

I also want to thank my daughter Maria and her family for providing me with the computer and getting it set up for me so I was able to get this all recorded. And for helping me out when I got stuck and didn't know how to fix the mess I got my self into.

I hope you will all enjoy this little bit of history about the family and maybe it will bring back some memories for you about other things that happened when we were kids growing up in Fountain.

I have been asked if I had an email address, now that I have a computer. The answer is NO. I may be dumb but I am not stupid. I don't need the hassle of worrying about some hacker getting in to my computer and stealing my personal information or my identity or getting all that SPAM that I have heard about. Maybe some day I will change my mind but for the time being, no email.

Chapter One
Oscar Davison Family

      I was asked if I remembered some of the places that we lived when we were growing up in Mason County and what I remembered about things when we were kids. So here are some of my memories and some of the things that others have told me about. To the best of my recollection, these are all true accounts of what happened.

      Retta Marie Bell, age sixteen, and Oscar Vinson Davison, age twenty four, were married on December 2, 1928 at Grandpa and Grandma Davison's home on the Mills farm in Sherman Township; two miles west and a half mile south of Fountain. Oscar found work in Grand Rapids and they lived there a short time before moving back to the Fountain area. The next couple of years were spent in various locations around the Fountain area. I understand they spent part of one winter living in a tar paper shack in the woods while Oscar was cutting wood or working in a sawmill. Oscar worked at different jobs. At one time he worked in the hardware store for Fred Reek and I think he was working there when George was born in March of 1930. They were living in a small house in Fountain at the time. Sometime later that year they moved back in with Grandma and Grandpa on the farm. I don't for sure remember just when or for how long.

      The summer of 1931 they were living in a tent near Elmer and Ginnie Vansickle's farm while Oscar worked on the thrashing machine and did various odd jobs. We all called her Aunt Ginnie even though she was no relation to us. She was there when George, Donna, and Marie were all born and helped in the delivery. She took care of them and Retta until Retta could get back on her feet.

One day, or so the story goes, Retta and Ginnie were visiting while George and Ginnie's niece, Irma, were playing in the kitchen. They took all the pots and pans out of the kitchen cabinet and Irma crawled inside and George locked her inside. He made it up to her later; he took her to the prom when they were juniors in high school.

In 1933 we were living just west of Fountain on what is now the Mathew's farm. That is where we were living when Donna was born in May of 1933. Oscar worked on the thrashing machine and in the sawmill for Elmer Van Sickle. George helped Oscar build a garage out of scrap lumber that Oscar brought home from the sawmill. It didn't keep all the rain and snow off the car but it helped, keeping most of it off. One day Oscar was planting potatoes and George was sent out to get him for lunch. On the way back to the house George was carrying the potato planter and jabbing it in the ground as they walked and he hit himself right on top of the foot. He was barefoot and couldn't afford shoes in those days; he still has a scar on top of his foot.

Our next move was to a place a mile and a half east and a half mile south of Fountain. I am not sure when we moved there but I know we were there part of the summer of 1934 and until the spring of 1935. That is where we were living when Marie was born in February of 1935. It was right on the banks of the Lincoln River and Oliver Loxson and his oxen[1] lived on

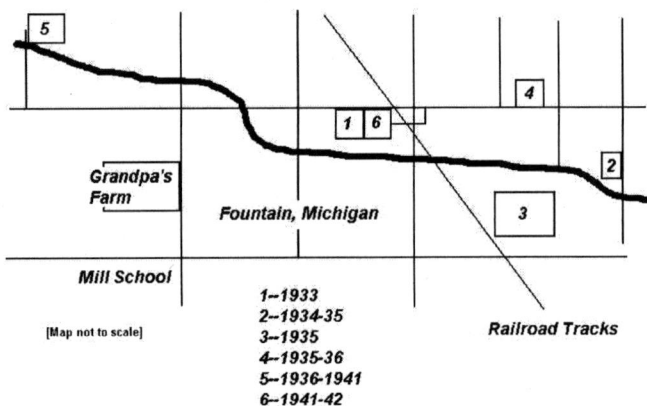

the other side of the river and across the road from us. He was the only farmer in Mason County to use a team of oxen. The house we lived in was later purchased by Red McCormick and moved into Fountain where he fixed it up and it became his home. When we were living there George had a pet duck and one cold winter night it went into the barn to get warm and one of the cows laid down on it and killed it. Retta had a china cabinet with a curved glass door and she put some gum on the top shelf so George wouldn't get it. Well, George wasn't going to let that stop him so he climbed up on the china cabinet to get the gum and tipped it over on top of himself and broke the glass in the door and some of the dishes. So if anyone remembers Retta having a china cabinet with no door and wondered why, now you know.

---

[1] Edtor's Note: The author is perfectly serious.

In the spring of 1935 we moved to a farm a mile south and a half-mile east of Fountain. The house was right beside the railroad tracks. That is were we were living when George started school. He would walk down the railroad tracks with the Yanus sisters who were a little older than he was. Every afternoon when the train went by on the way to Manistee, George would go out and wave to Billy Mason, the engineer. George got his first jackknife and one day he was using it to cut grass for the rabbits and it slipped and he cut himself on the forehead. That is the story he told his Mother and Father; actually, he was whittling on the back door casing when the knife slipped and he cut himself.

When the crops were all in that fall we were on the move again.

We spent the winter of 1935-1936 in a little house Wally Blohm owed about three quarters of a mile east of Fountain. A small creek ran right by the driveway. That is where Marie learned to walk. The floor in the house was so uneven and had such a slant to it that when we went to Grandma house Marie couldn't walk on a floor that was level. We lived there until the end of May and moved between May 25th 1936 and June 1st . The reason I remember these dates so well is that Fountain school didn't close until after June 1st and we moved to the Mill school district, which closed on May 25th. So George never got to finish kindergarten. Later he was able to convince people he had a college degree but the truth is he never finished kindergarten. Guess that is why he is so dumb.

The next five years May 1936 to June 1941 were spent on the Bowlie farm, 3 miles west and a half-mile north of Fountain. That is were we were living when Wayne was born in October of 1938. I guess he thought he was special because he was born in the hospital in Ludington instead of being born at home like the rest of us were. The first year there, George walked two and a half miles to Mill school and back every day. One fall day on the way home it was so cold and freezing George got so cold he began crying. Oscar was digging potatoes south of the house right by the road and he heard George coming about a half mile away. He thought George was singing but he was crying instead. When George got to the field where Oscar was working, Oscar told him to leave his books and lunch pail there and to run the rest of the way home to get warmed up.

The next year George got a bicycle to ride to school and Donna rode on the cross bar. When George got his bicycle he couldn't reach the pedals from the seat so we took the seat off and wrapped a grain bag around the cross bar and used it for a seat until his legs got long enough to reach the pedals. When we got the bicycle we took it over to Grandma's one day and Cleo, Glee, and Buster were watching some cattle feed in a hay field next to the road. George took his bicycle out there and they all took turns riding it down the hill and pushing it back up until they learned to ride it good enough to try riding it on the road. They all leaned to ride a bicycle that day.

On the way home George wanted to ride his bicycle so Oscar stopped about a mile from the house and George took off. He was doing real well until he tried to turn the corner from the main road onto the road that went to the house. He forgot to slow down and ran right in to a barb wire fence. He didn't get hurt but he scratched some paint off his brand new bicycle.

One summer Oscar got a job as foreman for a crew digging ditches for the WPA. I think that stood for "Workers Playing Around." Anyway, about once a month the crew and their families would come over to our house and we had a large front room we couldn't afford to furnish. So we used it for a dance hall. Some of them played musical instruments and Retta played the piano and some one would bring a keg of beer and they would have a big party.

For our entertainment we would go to the free movies put on by the merchants in Fountain or in Freesoil. On Sundays we would go to watch Oscar play baseball for the Fountain team. Then, we got our first radio. We didn't have any electricity so it was battery powered by a six volt car battery. We had a wind charger on the roof to recharge the battery. All the neighbors came over to listen to the fights and the ball games. Of course we had to listen to TOM MIX, THE LONE RANGER, FIBBER McGEE & MOLLY, THE SHADOW, JACK ARMSTRONG, THE ALL AMERICAN BOY, and JACK BENNY, just to name a few that I remembered.

Marie turned in to a problem child; one day she simply disappeared. We called and called and looked and looked all over for her and couldn't find her anywhere. We were all afraid she had gone down to the river and fallen in. Then someone looked in the car and there she was fast asleep on the back seat. She just got tired and decided to take a nap. Another time she climbed up to the loft in the barn. How she got up there no one knows, she was only two or three years old. When Oscar started up the ladder to get her, she said "Here, Daddy, catch" and tossed him an egg she had found in a nest up there.

Donna and George were playing cowboys one day and Donna ran around the corner of the barn. When George came around the corner after her she hit him over the head with the barrel of the gun and just about knocked him out. She said "That's the way the cowboys do it in the movies." Some how we all managed to survive, I don't know how but we did.

Of course, we had all the modern convenience of that time, like the old two-seat outhouse with bees buzzing around in the summer time. One day George was in the outhouse when a big bumblebee landed on the waistband of his pants. George didn't see it and when he started to pull his pants up the bee got him you know where. George was out the door and half way across the yard before he got his pants up. We also had honey bees under the house. Oscar went down in the basement and cut out a section of the molding and built a box over it for the bees to use for a hive and we had all the fresh honey we could use as long as we lived there.

One winter it was so cold we had trouble keeping the house warm with the old wood stove. So we closed the main part of the house and all moved into the basement. It was crowded but we kept warm and made it through the winter. The house was built on a hill with the south side of the hill cut away so we could go in and out the basement without going up and down stairs.

We had an electric fence around the pigpen; it was low voltage powered by a car battery. So one day George was going to check to see if it was working. He didn't want to touch it and get shocked so he touched it with a wooden stick; nothing happened. So he picked up a small iron rod and touched the fence with it--a shocking experience. I told you he was dumb didn't I?

One day Oscar, George, Donna and Marie went out to the pasture to drive the horses back to the barn. They were across the river so on the way back Oscar took Donna and Marie and crossed the river on a footbridge upstream from where the horses could cross and George followed the horses and waded across the river after them. One of the horses stopped so George walked up behind him and hit him with a short stick. The horse didn't like that so he kicked George right in the stomach and sent him rolling end over end. George was lucky, if he had been hit a little higher it could have crushed his chest or a little lower. Who knows.

We couldn't raise enough hay on the Bowlie farm to feed all our livestock so we would have to buy hay or put up hay on shares with another farmer. The summer of 1939 or 1940, when George was 9 or ten years old, Oscar had an agreement with Albert Beebe to cut and put up the hay on his farm, which was two miles east of Fountain. George would start out

out in the morning with a wagon, driving the team of Silver and Scout for the five-mile trip to Beebe's farm while Oscar did the milking and other chores around the farm. Then Oscar would follow with the car and another wagon. They would put two loads of hay in Beebe's barn then load up two more loads to take home. Oscar would take one load home with the car and George would make the five-mile trip back home with the horses and another wagonload of hay.

There were always plenty of things for us kids to do around the farm: feed chickens, slop hogs, milk cows, and gather eggs. In the summer there was the garden to take care of, and string beans and pickles to pick. They were our cash crop, which we sold to the canning factory. We would go swimming and take our bath in the Lincoln River. In the winter we would take our bath in the wash tub in the kitchen, if we took a bath at all. Didn't think much about B.O. back then. Since George was the oldest, he had more chores than the rest. Besides milking the cows, he had to help clean the barn, feed the cows and horses, and in the winter, spent hours pumping water by hand for all the livestock. We didn't sell the milk; we had an old cream separator that we had to turn by hand that would separate the cream from the milk. We would sell the cream and feed the skim milk to the hogs and calves.

Most of our food came from the farm: fresh milk and eggs delivered daily by our cows and chickens, fresh fruit and vegetables from our orchard and garden in the summer time, and Retta would can some for the winter months. Every fall we would butcher a pig and make our own bacon and lard. If Oscar could kill a deer, at night, on the back forty, we would have fresh venison. Or we would kill a calf or a cow in the fall. We would have to keep the meat hanging in the barn to keep it from spoiling since we didn't have any way to refrigerate it. Retta would can some of it for the summer. If we wanted chicken, we couldn't run down to the KFC, so we would just catch a chicken and chop its head off and have a chicken dinner. We grew our own potatoes and Navy beans, and we churned our own butter. We also got some food from a government surplus food program. I don't remember what all we got but I remember getting some canned meat and cornmeal. Retta would make johnnycake out of the corn meal and some times our supper would be johnnycake and milk. We didn't go hungry; we always had enough to eat.

    I found some corn bread at the bakery and had johnnycake and milk for supper last night before writing this section of the book.

    Before we leave the Bowlie farm I want to pass along a story I heard about one of our neighbors. I don't know how true it is but anyway, he had a horse for sale and his daughter got real upset when he put a sign up out by the main road that read "HORE FOR SALE." Sometimes, spelling was important.

    The spring of 1941 Oscar decided to give up farming and try to make his fortune in the big city of Muskegon. So, he had an auction and sold off his entire farm equipment and livestock except for a couple of cows he kept so we could have our own milk. He went to Muskegon and got a job at the Brunswick. He made a down payment on a forty-acre farm on the outskirts of Fountain.

In June of 1941 we were ready to move into a place of our own, a forty acre farm one quarter of a mile west of downtown Fountain, just inside of the village limits. If I remember right we were getting ready to move when Retta went into labor with Karla so they took her to the hospital in Ludington where Karla was born in June of 1941. When Retta and Karla came home we were all moved.

We now had our first house with electricity and central heating, an oil stove in the center of the living room that would burn all night instead of a wood burning stove that always went out during the night. We still didn't have running water until we drilled a new well and put in an electric pump and we still had an old two seat outhouse but it was ours. The well that was there when we moved in was down the hill about fifty yards from the house in a spring and we had to carry the water to the house in a bucket. We didn't want to drink that water so we got our drinking water from the neighbors. After we drilled a new well, Oscar told George to go down and take the pump off the old well and see if he could pull out any of the old pipe. When George pulled out the old pump and pipe all that was there was about two feet of pipe and the well point which was about three feet long setting in a barrel buried in the spring. I am glad we didn't drink that water, there were always snakes and frogs and toads swimming around in that barrel in that spring.

Oscar drove back and forth from Muskegon every weekend to be with the family until the war broke out in December of 1941. After the war broke out they started to ration gasoline and Oscar had trouble getting enough gas to come home every weekend. He would buy gas coupons from some of his coworkers, who didn't use all they were allotted, or get coupons from his brother, Clayton, and Grandpa if they had extra. Even then he couldn't make it every week. Sometimes when he was short of gas he would buy what gas he was allotted and then add five gallons of fuel oil that we were supposed to use to heat the house and take off for Muskegon in a cloud of smoke. That old car smoked like a coal burning locomotive, but it always got him back to Muskegon in time to go to work without blowing a gasket.

That winter Oscar brought a horse to use in the spring when he got ready to put in a garden. One day George rode it down town to get the mail and a loaf of bread. On the way home the horse decided he wanted to run and it was all George could do to hang on. He stayed on until he got to the driveway and the horse went north and George went south right in to a pile of snow. George hung on to the mail and the loaf of bread all right but the bread was kind of squished. Try holding a loaf of bread under your arm and squeezing it as tight as you can and see what you get. When Oscar came home that weekend and we told him what had happened. He told George to try riding the horse again only this time take him away from town because maybe a car or something had frightened him. So George rode the horse out to the cemetery which was about a half a mile west and turned around and started home and as soon as he started home the horse took off again. George held on until he got to the driveway and the horse decided to take a short cut over a snow bank. The horse went down on his knees and George slid right over his head into a puddle of water, it was spring and the snow was just starting to melt. The horse got up and trotted out to the barn and just stood there. So Oscar tried to ride him, he would be all right as long as they were going away from the barn but every time Oscar would turn and start back to the barn the horse wanted to run and it was all Oscar could do to hold him. I guess he just wanted to stay in the barn.

We went to a farm auction and purchased a sleeping sofa, the kind that the back folded down to make into a flat bed. When we got it home George wanted to sleep on it the first night. He didn't get much sleep, the bed bugs were there first and they kicked him out of bed. The sofa was infested with bed bugs and we had to fumigate the whole house to get rid of them.

One day when George was supposed to be milking the cows he started playing around in the barn with matches. Setting cobwebs on fire and ended up setting the barn on fire. The neighbors and some people passing by saw the smoke and came to help put out the fire before it could cause too much damage. It was a scary few moments for George.

When we first moved into the farm the house was in need of some repairs and if you remember Oscar wasn't too handy at that kind of work. So one of his co-workers, Fred Gley, came up to help him fix up the house. I will not go into any more detail on that matter but as you all know one thing led to another and our lives were changed forever because of that.

In the fall of 1942 Oscar was able to find an apartment in Muskegon at the Rudermen terrace housing project and we all moved to Muskegon just before school started in September. That is where we spent the next two years until the summer of 1944.

Donna also wanted to know about Oscar's baseball playing days with the Fountain baseball team. She wanted to know what position he played and what was the last year he played with the team.

Everyone talks about Vern being a good pitcher with the team; they seem to forget that Oscar was a pitcher too. I was talking with Wally Blohm one day and he said that he used to catch both Oscar and Vern when they were younger and that although Oscar didn't throw as hard as Vern, Oscar had better control and more movement on his breaking pitches. He thought Oscar was just as good a pitcher as Vern. I never saw Vern pitch because he moved to Grand Rapids before 1930 and didn't play for Fountain after that. One summer when I was about six or seven years old, Vern was playing with a team from Grand Rapids and they came up to Manistee to play a game. Oscar took me with him to see them play. Vern was playing second base that day; I had always heard about what a great player Vern was so I was looking forward to see him play. Well, they hit a slow rolling ground ball to him that was an easy double play ball and Vern let it roll right between his legs out in to short right field and he had to run it down. Everybody was safe and I remember thinking even I could have caught that ball. I guess even the great players' make an error now and then.

I don't remember Nelson playing for Fountain. He moved to Traverse City in 1936 so I wasn't old enough to remember watching him play. I know he played but I don't know what position he played or when he played for Fountain. The same is true for both Clayton and Whitman. I understand that they were both catchers but I never saw them play. Grandpa Davison was also a catcher in his younger days and I understand that he played his last baseball game on his fiftieth birthday.

I think that the last year Oscar played for Fountain was in 1940. He went to work in Muskegon the summer of 1941 and didn't have time to play ball that year and that was the last year they had a team because of the war. Then after the war in the summer of 1946 Oscar was instrumental in getting a team together and helped getting a league formed. He managed and pitch for the team the summer of 1946 and the next year, in 1947, he turned the team over to Jack Budzynski to manage and Oscar played with the team that summer but that was the last year he played.

There were four teams that made up the core of the league, Fountain, Freesoil, Riverton, and Carr Settlement. They were in the league year after year. Some of the other teams that were in the league, but not every year, were Custer, Baldwin, Irons, and Crystal Valley.

Some of the diamonds we played on were not the best fields for baseball. In Riverton there was a schoolhouse in right field any balls hit off the schoolhouse were considered a ground rule double, and anything hit over the schoolhouse was all you could get. The right fielder played with his back right up against the schoolhouse. In Carr Settlement the field was in a cow pasture, you had to be careful where you stepped and the field wasn't very level, first base was higher than third base and when you were making a throw from third to first you were throwing up hill.

The diamond in Fountain had a small slope behind second base and it looked like the center fielder was standing in a hole. Charlie Hansen use to play center field and I remembering seeing him scoop up a ground ball that was hit over second base and then turn and start running down the hill like he had missed it and it had gone between his legs. The batter couldn't see where the ball was so he would start for second base and Charlie would turn and throw the batter out at second. I saw him do that more than once.

During the 1930's the team from Fountain was sponsored by the merchants in Fountain and were known as the Fountain Merchants, they provided the team with uniforms and equipment. The uniforms didn't have the players name on them, instead they had the name of some of the business that paid for the uniforms. You would see names like BLOHMS GARAGE, SCHOENHERR LUMBER CO., ADAMS GROCERY, FOUNTAIN TAVERN, MICKEVICH GARAGE, REEK HARDWARE, and BRANDT'S MEAT MARKET on the uniforms; just to name a few that I remembered.

Paul Schoenherr was the team manager and when the team played away from Fountain he would use his truck from the lumberyard to haul the players to the game. They would all pile onto the back of the truck and away they would go. I remember going with them when I was a kid.

Some of the players that made up the team between 1935 and 1940 and the positions they played the most were:

CLYDE WAITE..........CATCHER, FIRST BASE
SLIM LEONARD.........FIRST BASE, PITCHER
BERNIE ANDRULES...............SECOND BASE
HENRY SCHOENHERR............. SHORTSTOP
JOE BUDZYNSKI........................THIRD BASE
CHARLIE HANSEN.................CENTER FIELD
ED BUDZYNSKI............PITCHER, OUT FIELD
MIKE BUDZYNSKI........................OUT FIELD
DON BUDZYNSKI..........................OUT FIELD
HOWARD CHATFIELD....................CATCHER
OSCAR DAVISON........PITCHER, OUTFIELD
and just about every position they asked him to, including CATCHER.

There were other players that came and went during that period of time but these were the players that made up the core of the team between 1935 and 1940. Of course, almost all the players would play more that just one position and they would move around as needed.

Chapter Two
Growing up in Michigan – The Teen Years

In the fall of 1942 just before school started we moved in to the Rudderman Terrace housing project in Muskegon. Each set of apartments in the project was set in a quad with four to six apartments in each building. We were lucky to get an apartment on the end of the building so we only had neighbors on one side. The walls were paper-thin and you could hear the people in the adjoining apartment, so we had to adjust our life style and not play the radio too loud and not yell at each other or the neighbors would hear us. It was a two-story apartment with the kitchen dining area and a large living room on the first floor, along with three bedrooms and the bath upstairs. The Tumulis boys, Pete, Tony, and Bill, who lived across the road from us when we lived on the Bowlie farm, all stayed with us at one time or another while we lived there. Wayne, my brother who still lives in the area, said that they tore down the apartments in the project in 2001 or 2002.

George found that he had more free time now that he didn't have cows to milk and farm chores to do so he had more time to pursue other interest like girls and sports. He wasn't very successful with the girls although he did have a crush on Bonnie Pipper, a voluptuous blond who lived in the same quad. So did about fifty other boys who lived in the housing project. He had about the same chance with her as a snowball in Phoenix in the summertime. So he spent more time playing baseball and football with her brother Tommy.

George didn't play much football growing up on the farm and in Fountain, there were never enough boys around, so that fall he got to find out what football was all about. Every weekend and most afternoons after school you could always find a football game going on. There was no Pop Warner or organized teams, no coaches, no referees, no parents cheering on the sidelines, just a bunch of boys beating on each other. We didn't play tag or flag football either, we played plain old hard nose, smashmouth, tackle football with no helmets, or pads and you know what? No one ever got hurt either, no concussions, no broken bones. Maybe a few bruises and some black and blue marks or a skinned up knee from sliding on the hard ground but no serious injuries. Just a group of boys out to have a good time. Some time there might be only four or five boys on each side, other times there could be as many as ten or twelve on each team just depending on how many showed up and got together.

One Saturday afternoon, one of the boys from the project arranged for a pickup game with a group of good old boys from a nearby Catholic school. On one play George was lined up on the line and he noticed the boy lined up against him pick up a hand full of dirt just as they got set, but he didn't think anything about it. When the ball was snapped, George got a hand full of dirt thrown in his face. On the next play one of the older and bigger boys on our team lined up against that boy to teach him a lesson. Those good old Catholic altar boys weren't very nice. If I remember right I think they beat us pretty good that day too.

That winter George kept busy with activities at the recreation center at the project. They had dances and other activities most of the time. George also joined the boy scouts and was a den leader for a pack of cub scouts. On weekends George might take the bus down town to go to the movies and some times he would go watch the professionals wrestlers. They were real wrestlers like you would see if you went to a high school or college wrestling match today. Not that fake stuff you see on TV now.

One night at the wrestling matches one of the wrestlers got his opponent in a leg hold and was twisting his leg to get him to give up. He twisted it so hard that he broke the leg. When that leg broke, you could hear the bone crack all over the arena. We all felt so sorry for the guy that got his leg broken because he wasn't even supposed to be in the ring that night; he was filling in for another wrestler who canceled just before the match. One of the wrestlers went by the name of the Human Blimp, about six hundred pounds of pure fat. He would do all right as long as he could stay on his feet but once they got him down on the mat he was all done. He was so fat he couldn't get back up on his feet. The only way he could get up was to roll over under the ropes to the edge of the ring and then sit up. Then they would have to get him a stool or a set of steps to stand up on to get back in the ring. They said that at one time he was so big that they had to use a hoist to get him into the ring. I don't know how true that was because when I saw him he was able to climb into the ring by himself.

In the spring of 1943, George's beloved Detroit Tigers came to Muskegon to play an exhibition game with a farm team they had in Muskegon. Of course George couldn't miss a chance to see the Tigers play and he had to go to the game. The Tigers had a power hitting first baseman by the name of Rudy York and every time he came to bat you could tell he was swinging for the fences trying to hit a home run. He would get up there and swing just as hard as he could at every pitch, I don't think he hit the ball out of the infield all day. Later in the game the Tigers put in Dizzy Trout, a good hitting pitcher and a fan favorite to play second base. He was a real clown always doing some crazy things and acting up in the field. When he came to bat he stood in the batters box twirling the bat around like a baton and when the pitcher threw the ball he took a nice easy swing and hit the ball out of the park for a home run. Just goes to show you that it's not how hard you swing the bat but how solid you make contact with the ball that counts.

Now that winter was over and it was spring, that only meant one thing to George— *BASEBALL*. After school, on weekends and all summer long you would find George with his glove and bat looking for a ball game somewhere. Oscar had a catcher mitt and mask and George would take them with him because he knew that most of the kids didn't like to catch but George didn't care, he would catch or play anywhere just as long as he got to play. Some times they would just play work up if they didn't have enough for two teams. In work up you got to play every position. If you were a batter and when you made an out you would go out to right field. When the next batter made an out you moved to center field, then to left field, then to third base, shortstop, second base, first base, pitcher, catcher and then back to batter again. When more kids showed up and we had enough for two teams we would choose up sides and have a game. Sometimes we would play all day long or until it got too dark to see the ball.

In the fall of 1943 George went to Bunker Junior High School. It was a new experience for George who was use to a small school and having the same teacher for all his classes. Now he had a different teacher for each class and had to get use to going from one room to another after each class. He got lost a few times the first week but somehow managed to get to all his classes--maybe a little late—but he got there. It was there that George got introduced to basketball; he didn't play on the team but got to play in PE and learned a little bit about the game, how to dribble, pass, and shoot the basketball. It all helped him make the basketball team later when he got to high school. In the spring of 1944 they had a citywide track meet.The boys were put in different classes, based on their age, weight and height. George won a ribbon for third place in the shot put in his class.

Coming home from school in the wintertime the kids would take a shortcut and cross a small creek on the ice, which was between the school and the project. It was frozen over just about all winter long. One day late in the winter George was leading the way and was the first one to start across when the ice broke and George fell in to the creek. One of the factories, a foundry, dumped their waste into the creek upstream and that water was putrid, it really stunk. George was wearing an old, heavy, army wool trench coat and boy did it smell when George got home. I don't think we ever got the smell completely out of that coat. After that we took the long way home for the rest of the school year.

One day Donna was doing the dishes and she climbed up on a chair to put some dishes away in the cupboard above the stove. Her dress caught fire and she got burned real bad. She missed about a month of school and they didn't pass her so she had to repeat the fifth grade.

In the spring of 1944, George had his first train ride and made his first trip out of the state of Michigan. One week end, Fred Gley took him to Chicago, a small berg on the southwest corner of Lake Michigan. The people down there thought that they were part of the United States and that Michigan was a foreign country. Most of them didn't even know where Michigan was. George got to meet Fred Gley's brothers and sisters and went to a ball game with some of his nephews. Can't remember now if it was the Cubs or the White Sox.

When Fred Gley returned from his tour of duty in the south Pacific and came back to Muskegon after being discharged from the army the relationship between Retta and Oscar got real bad. In the spring of 1944 Oscar moved out of the apartment and went to live with his brother Clayton. Retta and the kids stayed in the apartment. As soon as school was out George packed up and went back to Fountain to stay with Grandma and Grandpa Davison. At the time, the plan was to spend the summer there and come back to Muskegon when school started. But one weekend Oscar went over to the apartment to see the kids and Retta was gone and Donna, Marie, Wayne and Karla were there by themselves. Oscar packed the kids up and brought them all up to Fountain for Grandma to take care of. When the divorce was finalized later that year, Oscar was able to get custody of the kids and left them in the care of Grandma.

It was a little crowded when we all moved in with Grandma and Grandpa. They only had a two bed room house and Grandma had three foster kid she was taking care of for the county. The county found a new foster home for two of them right away but Raymond Curry, who had been with Grandma for about eight years since he was about six or seven years old, stayed with us awhile longer until he was old enough to go live with his father. We had to sleep on a rollaway bed and a sleeping sofa in the living room. So the first thing we had to do when we got up in the morning was to make our beds. There was a building in back that used to be a garage and George would sleep there in the summer time. We had a wood stove in the garage so we could sleep there in the winter time too if we had to. George and

Oscar would sleep there in the winter when Oscar came up from Muskegon until Grandpa had it moved around to the side of the house and started using it for a garage again. At first we had to use the outhouse out back but later Grandpa put a small addition on the house and added a bathroom with a shower and running water. We had chickens so we had fresh eggs and Grandpa planted a large garden so all summer long we had sweet corn, tomatoes and other fresh vegetables and potatoes. A year or two later Grandpa got a couple of cows so we could have fresh milk. George had to start milking cows again. Bill Goff needed pasture for his cows and we needed a place closer to the house to keep our cows, so Grandpa and Bill Goff entered in to some kind of agreement. They fenced in our forty acre farm and used the whole farm for pasture in the summer and in the winter we kept our cows in Bill Goff's barn and he provided the hay for the cows.

The summer of 1944, George's aunt and uncle, Iva and Don Royal, wanted to take a vacation. Because it was during the war and gas was rationed, they had to figure out a way to get extra gas to make the trip. One of the ways they could do that was to sign up to help the farmers harvest their crops. One of Iva's cousins owned a cherry farm in northern Michigan, near Traverse City, so they signed up to pick cherries. They took Don's youngest brother along and they picked George up on the way. They went up to Elk Rapids, which is on the east shore of Grand Traverse Bay. Another one of Iva's cousins owned a large resort hotel right on the edge of the bay. The hotel was closed but they had two or three small cottages on the property and we stayed in one of them. During the week we would go out and pick cherries until the middle of the afternoon and then we would go back to town and spend the evening swimming in the bay and just loafing around. I guess you have to call it a working vacation, but we still had fun.

I guess that when gasoline is rationed and hard to get people will go to extreme measures just to get somewhere. I heard of two families that got together one summer to go on vacation and they got into two cars. One car would tow the other car for a while then they would switch and the other car would tow the other one. They kept switching back and forth until they got to where they were going. Of course during the war there wasn't much traffic on the road, I wouldn't want to try it now with all the traffic and the speeds that people drive but back then you could probably do it with out much of a problem. I don't know how much gas they saved by doing that but I guess you wouldn't use as much gas as you would if you were driving both cars.

One week during haying season that summer George got a job driving horses for Clarence Chatfield and his boys, Howard and Sheldon. It wasn't hard work, all you had to know was "giddyup," "whoa," "gee" and "haw" and try and keep the wagon straddle of the windrow when picking up the hay. It helped if you had a good loud voice, which George had, so the horses could hear you. The best part of the job, as far as George was concerned, was that he also got dinner and supper and Mrs.

Chatfield could cook. Home made bread and biscuits and fresh baked homemade pie or cake for every meal and her boys could eat too. There was nothing skinny or lean about any of them.

Another job that George had that summer was picking string beans and pickles. The harder you worked the more money you made, because you were paid by the pound. Some days George would make good money and other days he would fool around more and not do so good. He also worked in Daly's orchard picking dewberries and gooseberries; again he got paid by the quart so the more he picked and the less he ate the more money he made. Erma Daly who was in charge of the workers knew how George liked to fool around and goof off so when she could she would pair him up with one of the older retired men who worked there to make some extra money. When George was working with him he would make a good day's wage, other days he would just make a little pocket change. That fall after school and on Saturdays he would work for some of the farmers picking up potatoes. One of the men would dig the potatoes and George would follow along behind and pick up the potatoes, again he was paid by the bushel so the harder he worked the more he would make.

The summer of 1945 George and Freddie Mathews both got jobs on a dairy farm, north of Kings' corners and west of Freesoil. They would have to get up early every morning to go get the cows in the pasture and bring them to the barn then they would have a cup of coffee before they started milking, after the milking was done they would have breakfast and then start the day's work. The farmer they worked for had a hay baler and they would travel all over the county baling hay for other farmers. It took four people to operate the baler, one to drive the tractor, one man stood on the baler and fed the hay into the baler. George and Freddie sat on the back end, one would feed the wire to tie the bales and the other would tie the wire when the bales got to the proper size. It was hot dirty work with all the dust and chaff from the hay. They had to wear goggles to keep the dirt out of their eyes and knowing what we know today they should have wore some kind of mask so they wouldn't breath all that dust but they didn't know at the time. Sometimes they would have to help load the bales on the wagons; that wasn't easy work either, throwing sixty to ninety pound bales of hay around. After haying was over George worked on the combine, bagging and tying bags of oats, rye, and wheat. That was just as bad as the baler was as far as the dirt and chaff was concerned and the bags were just as heavy. One day after completing a job on one of the neighboring farms we had two tractors and a truck to get back to our farm and only two drivers. It was only about three miles so George said that he could drive the truck if he had to; he was only fifteen. Well, about halfway home he turned his head to check to see if everything was all right on the back of the flatbed truck and went off the road into a ditch and just about rolled the truck over. All the tools and equipment on the truck went flying off and he was busy picking things up when the other hired man driving one of the tractors caught up to him. He helped George get everything back on the truck, then he drove the truck the rest of the way home and let Freddie drive the tractor. George was one frighten boy and thought he was going to get fired, but when we told the boss what happened he just laughed and said that there was no real harm done, but they didn't ask George to drive the truck again. I wonder why?

When George returned to school in Fountain the fall of 1944 to start his freshman year he rejoined three kids he had started kindergarten with nine years earlier: Wally Budzynski, Lois Williams, and Irma VanSickle, they were joined by Keith Eggerstedt who's father had just purchased a store in Fountain. The five of them made up the ninth grade at Fountain that year and the tenth grade the following year. Later, after the five of them transferred to Scottville High School for their junior and senior years someone at Scottville started calling them the Fountain Five because they were always together. When George went back to Scottville in 2003 for the class 55th reunion he was shocked to find out he was the only surviving member of the Fountain Five; the other four had all passed away.

The Fountain school was just a three room school with only three teachers. Harry McFarland taught the seventh, eighth, ninth and tenth grades all in the same room and all at the same time.

The classes weren't very big. The year George was in the ninth grade there were five in his class, the tenth grade had just three girls, the eighth grade was all girls, eight of them and the seventh grade was made up of seven boys and one girl. Mr. McFarland would have a math quiz and a spelling bee about once a month with all four grades. George would do all right with the math quiz but he was the worse speller in the whole school. When they had a spelling bee he would be the first one to set down; even the seventh and eighth graders would beat him. We had a shuffle board court painted on the floor on one side of the class room and in the winter time we would play shuffle board at recess and lunchtime. The township hall was right next door to the school and sometimes in the winter we would go over there to play basketball at lunchtime. The hall wasn't heated at all so sometimes it could get pretty chilly in there when we were playing. When we were in the tenth grade we had a basketball team made up of the three tenth grade boys and some of the eighth grade boys. We played the freshmen team from Scottville and Freesoil and had a couple of games with Carr Settlement, which was the only other school in the county that only went through the tenth grade. Of course George wanted to play baseball so in the spring of 1946, when he was in the tenth grade, he organized a team and talked Mr. McFarland into getting them a couple of games with Carr Settlement. There wasn't a lot of baseball talent in a school so small and we ended up with a 6th grader playing shortstop but we had a good time. Then, just before school was over we had a game with the Fountain old timers that played on the Fountain baseball team before the war. This time George got his dad Oscar to pitch and Mr. McFarland to play third base to start the game, then they switched part way through the game. George was the catcher; he didn't know any better.

The spring of 1946 the county decided to have a music festival for all the grade schools in the county. They sent a music director around to all the schools to help them prepare for the festival. The morning she was to come to Fountain Mr. McFarland told the ninth and tenth grade that, since it was only for the elementary school, they could go play softball when she got there. But when she got there she had a different idea, she wanted them to stay and take part in the program. When she gave them a break, George and Wally got a softball and a couple of bats and convinced most of the ninth and tenth graders to join them. They took off across the school grounds and went down the railroad tracks to an open field and played softball until noon then they came back to school. The kids that didn't go said that when we didn't come back after the break, the music director asked Mr. McFarland to go get us. They said he walked out the back door and looked around then came back and said they were gone and he couldn't find them. She wasn't mad or upset, she was livid. They said that she said, "Well, I will find them" and she went and got in her car and drove around town looking for them. She couldn't find them because the field they were in couldn't be seen from the road. I don't know if Mr. McFarland got in any trouble for what he did or not but he never said anything to any of us about it. We made it all up later when they had the music festival; the ninth and tenth grade from Fountain did a couple of square dances that stole the show. They had some pretty good square dancers in that group.

    Mr. McFarland was also the scoutmaster for a Boy Scout troop in Fountain and one day he told George to take a hike. One of the requirements for a merit badge that George was working on was a fourteen-mile hike. George and Freddie Mathews got together and planned to take a hike to Sable Station, which was about ten miles east of Fountain. That would make it about a twenty mile round trip which was more that enough to meet the requirements for the merit badge. They got their equipment all together pup tent, sleeping bags and food and took off one Saturday morning and got to Sable Station in the middle of the afternoon. They set up the tent and there was a lot of dry leaves around so they filled the tent over half full of dry leaves to make a nice soft place to sleep that night. After they had supper they crawled in the tent and went to sleep. When they got up the next morning they discovered that it had rained pretty hard during the night but neither one of them heard a thing. They also found a fresh deer track where a deer had walked past within five feet of their tent after the rain had stopped. After breakfast they started the long hike back to Fountain and got home late Sunday afternoon; two very tired boys too pooped to party.

    In the woods near Fountain there were a lot of pine stumps left from earlier logging and they made good kindling to start a fire with. Some of them had a lot of pitch pine in them and they would really burn hot and fast. One day, Mr. McFarland took the Boy Scout troop out to gather some kindling for the church in Fountain. They took along some hot dogs to roast for lunch and George took along a can of pork and beans. He wanted to warm them up for lunch so he put the can on the edge of the fire. They got warm all right but George didn't get to eat any of them. The can exploded and everyone got showered with beans. Before you put a can of anything on the fire to warm up, be sure you open the can first or at least punch an air hole in it to let the steam escape or you will get what George got, a big explosion.

That winter, George had the job of building the fire to warm up the church. The church had a large coal burning stove in the basement and George would have to get up early every Sunday and start a fire in the stove and hope it took the chill off before services would start.

When Mr. McFarland died a couple of years later, George was honored to be one of the pallbearers at his funeral. Mr. McFarland had gone fishing at Ford Lake one night and when he didn't come home they found his boat the next morning but no sign of him. Divers recovered his body and everyone thought he had fell overboard and drowned. The autopsy showed he didn't have any water in his lungs and that he died of a heart attack not of drowning.

That summer a family was staying at Blue Lake and a couple of boys were diving off a motor boat and somehow they both dived off at the same time and the boat got away. One of the boys made it to shore but the other one didn't. George went up there and helped searched for the body. It is an eerie feeling to be swimming around under water and see a light spot on the bottom of the lake and reach for it not knowing if it is a body or just sand on the bottom of the lake. The sheriff department found the body later using gaffing hooks.

The summer of 1946 George went to Muskegon with Oscar and stayed with his Uncle Clayton. George got a job in a small family owned grocery store, bagging groceries, carry out, stocking shelves, mopping floors, cleaning the store room and all the other chores you would expect to find in a grocery store. He worked there all summer until it was time for school to start, then he went back up to Fountain and started his junior year at Scottville High School.

Scottville High School served most of central Mason County, as a matter of fact years later, when they built a new school; they changed the name to Central Mason County High School. Most of the kids rode the bus to school. It was twelve miles from Fountain to Scottville but because the bus route had to zigzag back and forth to cover all the area between Fountain and Scottville, it was at least a twenty mile trip and took over an hour with all the stops and so on. Albert Beebe lived out by Ford Lake and was our bus driver. He kept the school bus at his place overnight and Fountain was his second pickup in the morning. One morning when George got up and started to fix his breakfast, he looked out the window and saw the school bus was already there. He wondered why the bus was there so early. About that time there was a knock on the door and it was Albert Beebe. He had set his alarm clock for an hour earlier that he wanted and didn't realized it until he got to town and no one was there waiting for the bus. Then he checked his watch and realized what had happened. He came in and had a cup of coffee with George until it was time to leave. One winter morning after a heavy snow the night before we started for Scottville before the snow plows had a chance to clear the roads. We only got about a mile out of town and Albert turned around and came back to Fountain and called the school and told them he couldn't make it because the snow was too bad. The snow wasn't so deep, only about a foot but it was a real wet heavy snow and the bus was really laboring to get through it. So we had a snow day off from school. Since we had such a long bus ride some times we would do our homework on the bus and have it all done by the time we got home. But then again we would spent a lot of time just goofing around and teasing the girls.

Because so many of the kids rode the bus to school and home again, the school had to adjust their athletic programs to accommodate them. Instead of having practice before or after school they used the last two periods of the day for practice. If you didn't go out for sports or if you got cut from the team you would spend the last two periods in study hall. At least the boys did. They had other classes the last two periods too, but most of the boys arranged their schedule so they would have those periods free for sports. Of course, on game days that was another story. If you were on the team you got home any way that you could after a game. You could always get a ride to Kings' Corners, which was seven miles north of Scottville on the highway. But the five miles from there to Fountain you just hoped that someone would come along and give you a ride. One night after a late basketball game in North Muskegon we were real late in getting back. After George got a ride to Kings' Corners he started walking and he had to walk every step of the way, five miles, back to Fountain. Not one car came along. It was a good thing it was a Friday night and he didn't have to get up and go to school the next day because he never would have made it. Sometimes when they got back from a game early George would go down to the pool hall and bowling alley to see if anyone from Fountain was there and catch a ride home with them. But that night it was so late and everything was closed, he didn't have any choice. That was the only night he had to walk the full five miles but other times he would walk three or four miles before he got a ride.

On nights when there was a football or basketball game, most of the kids went home after school and then came back to school when it was time for the game. George didn't have that option since he didn't have anyone to bring him back to school. So George and a couple of other boys who didn't have transportation would go down to the pool hall and get a hamburger for supper and shoot pool until it was time to go back to school. There wasn't any McDonalds or fast food restaurants to go to.

The athletic department didn't have a very big budget and when George went out for football he found he didn't have much of a choice for his equipment. The returning varsity players got first choice for the equipment and the new comers had to take what was left over. The only thing George had that fit him properly was his shoes, which he had to buy himself. Everything else was about 2 or 3 sizes to big, his shoulder pads, and hip pads were so big and bulky he could hardly move with them on. His junior year the coach had him try out at fullback but I don't think he even played in one game that year. His senior year they moved George to guard and he got to start one game. The other team ran the first two plays right over him for big gains and he spent the rest of the game and most of the rest of the season on the bench. Late in the season, in a game where we had a big lead, George and the rest of the subs got to play late in the 4th quarter. The other team had a big guard that was listed at 220 pounds; George was about 125 pounds. We had the ball and the first play they called was a run between guard and tackle. George was going to have to block that 220 pounds guard to make the play work. When the ball was snapped George charged across the line to make his block and just about fell flat on his face. That big tub of lard was back pedaling so fast to keep from getting hit that George never caught up with him. George didn't get a letter in football but he enjoyed the experience and he got out of study hall. We didn't have a very good football team. We lost more games than we won.

George made the basketball team in his junior year. He wasn't a starter but he got enough playing time to earn a letter. We did better in basketball that we did in football, we didn't win any championship but we had a good team and won more than we lost. In his senior year George was getting a little more playing time coming off the bench to start the season and was on his way to earning another letter. Then his Uncle Whitman got hurt in an accident on his farm and needed someone to help with the milking and chores on the farm. George couldn't keep playing basketball and be home in time to help him so George dropped off the basketball team. George had his driver's license now and could use Whitman's car to go back and forth to school but he wouldn't be able to make it when they had a game away. So it was back to study hall for George. He wasn't playing that much anyway but that ruined his chance to earn a second letter in basketball.

When baseball season came in his junior year, George won the starting job as catcher; he was also the leadoff batter in the lineup. We had a big tall pitcher who was about 6 feet tall and when he and George got together on the mound it was like Mutt and Jeff. The pitcher had a good fast ball and good control. George said he could catch him with his eyes closed, all he had to do was put the mitt where he wanted the ball and it would be there. We had a good team that year and tied for the conference championship with a record of 8 and 2. Much better than we did in other sports.

The spring of 1948, after losing 3 of our starters from the championship team of the year before to graduation, including our pitcher, the baseball team bounced back with the help of some underclass men who stepped up to the plate and filled in the gap. We had a sophomore pitcher who had fair control and a real good curveball, which most high school players weren't use to hittting. The first baseman was one of the best glove men I have ever played with but he couldn't hit if you let him bat with a bass fiddle. The coach also wanted George to get on base more because he was the lead off batter, so he told George that because he was good at getting the bat on the ball, he didn't want George to swing at any pitch until he had two strikes. George got real good at getting on base, he would take a walk, get hit by a pitch and get on base anyway he could. He raised his batting average about one hundred points over the year before. The coach didn't like it at all if you got called out on a third strike, he said that if it was close enough to be called a strike, it was close enough to hit so you got fined if you didn't swing at the third strike. It was all right if you swung at a pitch out of the strike zone but you better not let the umpire call strike three if you weren't swinging at the ball.

We went 10-0 that year and won the conference championship. The other schools in the conference were Hart, Shelby, Montague, Whitehall, and North Muskegon.

One day we were playing at Montague. Their pitcher was on second base and he was trying to score on a base hit. The throw to home was a little up the line toward third base and George moved a couple of steps toward third to get the ball. Just as the ball hit George's mitt, the runner hit George with a full head of steam. George went down and the ball squirted out of his mitt. George's baseball instinct told him the batter would be trying to go to second. So George got the ball and got up to throw to second, but when he stood up all he could see were white dots dancing around the

**1948 Scottville High School
Conference Champions**

infield. His head finally cleared enough so he was able to make out one of his teammates and George threw the ball to him. That pitcher weighed about 180 pounds and played fullback on their football team. George weighed about 130 pounds with all his equipment on. It was like a Mack truck hitting a Volkswagen. When the play was over George looked over at the bench and Tellie Knowles was putting on his catching gear. Tellie had been the backup catcher for two years and never got in a game and he thought sure this was his chance. But it wasn't to be; George stayed in the game. I guess the pitcher felt sorry for what he did because when George came to bat later in the game he threw him a fast ball, belt high, right down the middle. George took a mighty swing and he got it all, I mean he got all of it. There was a tennis court in deep left field with a backstop around it, like they have on most tennis courts. Any ball hit in to the backstop was a ground rule double, anything hit over the backstop was all you could get. Well George hit it over the backstop. He was rounding third base, sure that he had a homerun, when Bob Murphy, who was coaching third base, threw up his hands and yelled stop, and get back to third. George slipped and fell and dove back into third base, when he got up the ball was just coming in to the shortstop. He is sure he could have made it home if Murphy hadn't held him up. The center fielder had gone on to the tennis court to get the ball, the left fielder had gone over to center field to get the relay and the shortstop had gone out to short left field to get the relay from the left fielder. The next batter got a hit and George scored and we won the game but George never forgave Murphy for robbing him of the only homerun he ever hit in his long baseball career. It was his only triple too. When the coach handed out letters at the end of the season he said that George was the smallest but scrappiest catcher in the league.

Every year when they had the Oceana County fair at Hart, they had amateur boxing matches as part of their program. Most of the boxers came from gyms in Muskegon and Grand Rapids. The gym from Grand Rapids always had some real good boxers and usually won most of the championships. In 1946 Felix Mickevich got a group of boys together from

Mason County and gave them some boxing lessons and took them down to the fair at Hart and entered them in the boxing matches. George decided to give it a try. That year George weighted in at 122 pounds and fought in the featherweight division. He was only 16 years old and he was matched with an older fighter from Grand Rapids who was a Navy veteran and had boxed in the Navy. George gave it his best shot and went the full 3 rounds but lost a split decision. The amateur boxing matches were three, three minute rounds. George came out of that fight with one eye swollen shut but he was still standing when it was over. The next year, 1947, when George was 17 he was worried about making the weight limit so he didn't eat or drink before the weigh in and he weighted in at 120 pounds and they put him in the bantamweight division. He made it to the championship match that year and won a metal for runner up. He was one of only two boxers in his division that year. George didn't make it through the first round. He was knocked down twice and the referee stopped the fight and awarded the victory to the other fighter. It was recorded as a technical knock out in the first round. The paper said that George was knocked out with a blow to the solar plexus. George said that wasn't true "He hit me in the belly and knocked the wind out of me." George got right back up after each knock down and thought he could continue but the rules stated that two knock downs in a round and the fight would be stopped. So that was it and George gave up boxing after that. That winter George saw in the paper that the kid who beat him that night won the Bantamweight Golden Gloves championship for the state of Michigan. So he must have been a pretty good boxer.

In the spring of 1948 the letterman's club from Scottville High School got to go down to Detroit to Tiger Stadium to a baseball clinic the Tigers were putting on for the high schools in the state. The boys were divided into groups depending on the position they played and one of the players from the Tigers would talk to the boys and give them pointer's and tips on playing their position. For example, when a catcher is trying to catch a popup, he wants to get under the ball and then line the ball up with his nose, that way he is either going to catch it or it is going to hit him in the nose. You don't see very many catchers getting hit in the nose with a pop fly do you? After the clinic we got to watch batting practice and stayed for the game.

Most of the seniors went on a trip just before graduation. We took a school bus to Detroit and got on a cruise ship. We had a flat tire on the way and just about missed the boat. We had to send a couple of the kids ahead in a taxi to hold the boat for us. We were suppose to cruise Lake Erie and go to Niagara Falls but the dock workers were on strike where we were suppose to dock at Niagara Falls, so they wouldn't let us off the boat. So we spent 3 days and 2 nights cruising Lake Erie. Played a lot of blackjack to past the time away. There were students from other schools around the state on the cruise so we got to make some new acquaintances. We all enjoyed it even if we didn't get to see Niagara Falls.

Even though George spent so much time with his sports he managed to keep his grades up by taking easy classes and classes that he knew he could do well in; classes like advanced algebra, solid geometry, physics, speech and agriculture. He avoided the harder subjects like typing, Latin, chemistry, calculus, and trigonometry. So he was real proud when the class standings came out at the end of the year and he came home and told his family that he had graduated sixth in his class of forty-seven. His dad said "So what, I graduated sixth in my class too."

So George asked, "How many were in your class?" And his dad said, "Six."

Don't do any good to brag about yourself.

While living with Grandma and Grandpa, whenever George would stay out late on a Saturday night or come home late after a game at school, and no matter how late it was or how quiet he would try to be when he came in the house, the moment he walked in he would hear Grandma say "Is that you George?" He would answer "Yes Grandma, go back to sleep."

So he would try not to stay out too late too often. So it wouldn't surprise George at all if late some night as he tries to sneak through those Pearly Gates, when St. Peter isn't looking, to hear Grandma say "Is that you, George?" Of course to be realistic about it, when that time comes it won't be the Pearly Gates. He is much more likely to be greeted by Grandpa with some thing like, "It about time you got here boy, now grab a shovel and start shoveling that coal we have to keep this fire hot for those to follow." Who knows what will happen when that time comes?

George started smoking when he was 16; he would buy tobacco and roll his own cigarettes. He thought he was doing a good job of hiding it from Grandma and Grandpa until one day he and Grandpa was out on the farm checking the fences where they had the cattle. Suddenly Grandpa turned to George and asked, "What kind of tobacco do you have?" George was kind of shocked and didn't know what to say. Then Grandpa said, "I know you have some tobacco and I need a chew." So George handed him a pack of Old Bugler tobacco and Grandpa dug out a chew and handed the pack back to George. He didn't get after George for smoking and never said a word about George smoking. He just took his chew and they went on about the business at hand.

One summer George helped Grandpa build a rowboat. They took it to Thunder Lake and left it for the summer and some times George would ride his bicycle there and go fishing. He broke more cane poles that summer tying them to his bicycle and riding over those rough roads. He would come home with a nice mess of bluegills and perch and sometimes a bass. Grandpa would always say "What did you keep those little things for, I use them for bait." But after Grandma fried them you can be sure he ate his full share.

Oscar purchased a lot on Ford Lake and got an old two story house from a farm near Round Lake and had it moved to Ford Lake. It was about a six mile trip. George rode on top of the house to move any wires or other low hanging objects that we had to pass under. Just as we were coming out of the driveway of the farm where we had gotten the house, we had a telephone line to move. George was lifting the line to clear the roof of the house when he lifted it to high and it made contact with an electric wire that it passed under. George got a small shock and we blew an electric transformer. Probably the only thing that saved George is that the trailer and the tractor both had rubber tires. Otherwise he could have been knocked off the roof. He was real careful after that when he had to move any more wires and made the rest of the trip without any more problems.

George's First Car

They say there are some things in a person's life that they never forget. Like their first kiss, well George claims that he can't remember his first kiss but he will never forget his first car. A 1929 Chevrolet, it was older than he was. George got it right after he graduated from high school. When George brought it the starter didn't work so he had to crank it or push it to get it started. When he could he would park on a hill so he could roll down the hill and start it by putting it in gear. It was real easy to start. When he had to crank it the crank went through a slot in the bottom of the radiator. The crank would rub on the bottom radiator tank and after a while would cause the radiator to start leaking. George got tired of soldering the radiator so as soon as he could afford it he got a new starter for it.

The clutch plate was just about worn out. You had to let the clutch pedal just about all the way out before the clutch would engage. One night George and some of his buddies went out spotting deer. They were out in an open field and stopped when they thought they saw something, when they started up again George let the clutch all the way out and the car didn't move. George pushed the clutch pedal in again and this time he took his foot off real fast and let the clutch snap back. The car started moving and they didn't stop again until they got home. George got the clutch plate replaced the next week.

The gas gauge was on the gas tank on the back of the car, outside so you couldn't see it when you were driving. George was always running out of gas. Every time he ran out of gas the gas line would plug up with dirt and rust from the bottom of the gas tank. George would have to disconnect the gas line at the fuel pump and blow the dirt and rust out of the fuel line back into the gas tank.

    There was no window in the door on the driver's side. George had a piece of canvas that he hung over the window when he parked the car to keep the rain and snow out. He couldn't cover the window while he was driving so it got pretty cold in the wintertime. Of course, there was no heater either. So George would bundle up in a heavy coat and gloves and a hat with earmuffs to keep warm. The car had a wood frame around the doors and windows and a canvas roof with tar on it. The roof leaked causing the wood frame to rot out so the doors didn't always close tight. One day George went around a corner a little to fast. Wayne was with him and the door came open and Wayne just about fell out. Wayne was hanging on to the door for dear life. After that George tied the door shut with a leather strap. Another time George and Uncle Vern were going deer hunting. They were driving around the woods when the windshield slid out on to the hood. They just put the windshield in the back seat and went on with their hunting. When they got home they put the windshield back in place.

    The key had been broken off in the ignition switch, half of the key was in the ignition switch and the other half George kept on a string tied to the dash. The ignition switch was one of the kind that popped out when it was on so you only needed the key to turn it on. To turn it off you just had to push the switch in. So you never had to hunt for the key it was always handy.

George didn't worry about the car being stolen. Who was going to steal a twenty-year-old car that you had to crank to start?

Just after George got the car he took a few of his friends to the movies in Scottville one night. As they were leaving some one threw a firecracker as they were driving out of town. The police stopped them and wanted to know why they were always making the car pop and backfire every time they came to town. George told him that he had just got the car and it was the first time he had been to Scottville with it. The policeman let them go and George tried to make the car backfire all the way back to Fountain but couldn't make it backfire once.

Everywhere George went he always had a bunch of kids with him. They would go to the skating rink, to dances, to ballgames, out to the lake swimming or just riding around. In the fall they would go cooning, steal watermelons from the farms around town, or go hunting. When George worked in Muskegon he would drive back and forth to Fountain every weekend. A seventy-five-mile trip one way. That winter he worked on a farm near Kalamazoo, 160 miles from Fountain. He drove his car down there and when he got a few days off for Christmas he drove back up to Fountain and back again.

Christmas day George and Ernie Koviak went rabbit hunting. There had been a lot of snow and the roads were packed with snow and real slick and slippery. On the way home they came to the end of the road where they had to make a sharp right turn. George was going a little bit too fast and when he stepped on the brake and turned the wheel the car kept going straight ahead toward a big snow bank. Just as they hit the snow bank, George shifted into second gear and hit the gas. The car tipped up on two wheels and came back down and back on to the road. We came out of it with out getting stuck but just about rolled over. The only reason we didn't roll over is because the snow bank was so high. It was about 4 feet high where we hit it. George didn't like driving in the snow when the roads were so slick. In 2003 when George was in Michigan, over fifty years later he looked up Ernie and when they were talking Ernie asked George if he remembered the old '29 Chevrolet. Ernie said we sure had a lot of good times with that old car. So I guess George isn't the only one who remembers his first car.

    The brakes were never very good on that car. The rear brakes didn't work much at all and the front brakes were about all it had. When George went to Muskegon he use to stop and adjust the front brakes before he got in to heavy traffic. He would shift down in to lower gears to slow down and coast to a stop when he could. Some times if he was going real slow he would shift into reverse to stop. One day he was showing off and shifted into reverse when he was going to fast. The car stopped but he broke some teeth out of the gears in the transmission and snapped the drive shaft. That was the end of his BEAUTIFUL CAR. He sold the motor and the rest went for junk. But he sure had a lot of fun with that car in the year that he had it.

    After that he brought a 1934 Chevrolet from his Uncle Clayton. It wasn't near as much fun to drive as the old '29. But he still hauled a lot of his friends around in it and they had some good times. He sold that car to his Aunt Cleo when he went in to the Navy.

George Goes To Work

After George graduated from high school in 1948 he was expected to go to work to support himself. He went to Muskegon and boarded with his Uncle Clayton and Aunt Dorothy. He got a job at the Shaw Box Crane and Hoist Company. Yes they made all kinds of cranes and hoists. The big cranes like you see on construction jobs today to small hand operated hoist like you might find in a machine shop or garage. His first job was as a trucker. His truck was a wagon about two and a half feet wide and about five feet long. He would pull it all over the factory hauling small parts from one department or workstation to another. After about three months a job opened up as a drill press operator so George applied and got the job. It paid more, $1.20 a hour, big money at that time That job lasted until the first part of September when they had a slow down and started laying people off and George got laid off. None of the factories were hiring so George drew his unemployment pay until he could find another job.

While staying in Muskegon, George's cousins, Jackie and Phyllis, liked to go roller-skating at a rink in North Muskegon. They didn't have a car and George did so they talked George into going skating with them. George had never roller-skated before but he was willing to give it a try. At first he would just skate around the edge of the rink holding on to the railing or the wall. After a while he got brave enough to get out on the floor when they had free skating. He fell down a lot and was lucky he never got run over. One night when they were having what they called a trio skate, two boys and one girl or two girls and one boy skating together. Jackie and Phyllis talked George into skating it with them. Of course they had to hold George up to keep him from falling. About half way through the dance, George thought he was doing real good, then he got his feet tangled up and all three of them went down in a heap in the middle of the floor. They were lucky they didn't get run over. By the end of the summer George was getting better at it and was able to spend the night at the rink with out falling down.

  George went back up to Fountain and got a job on a large peach farm south of Ludington. He got his room and board and his main job was driving a tractor and trailer around the orchard picking up crates of peaches after they were picked. He would then take them to the barn and load them on the truck. When the truck was loaded he would take the truckload of peaches in to Ludington to the fruit exchange. That job lasted about a month until the peaches were all picked and shipped. Then it was back to drawing unemployment again. George wasn't in a hurry to find another job because it was getting close to deer season and he wanted time off to go deer hunting. So he got by with his unemployment check and just waited until deer season was over before he started look for another job.

George's Uncle LaVern Williams, George's mother's brother, was managing a large dairy farm down by Kalamazoo. When he heard George was out of work he offered George a job on the farm. So the first of December 1948, as soon as deer season was over George packed up his old '29 Chevy. and headed south about 160 miles to Kalamazoo. George spent the winter working there. Feeding and milking cows. Cleaning the barn, cutting wood, slopping the hogs, husking corn and other farm work. You may remember the old song, "I'VE GOT A GAL IN KALAMAZOO." Well, George was too busy working and he didn't have a Gal in Kalamazoo. George didn't like it at Kalamazoo. He was too far away from the rest of the family and his friends so that spring he quit his job and headed back up north to Fountain.

When George got back to Fountain he decided to try his hand at farming. The family had a forty-acre farm on the outskirts of Fountain but George didn't have any equipment. So he made an agreement with his Uncle Whitman, in exchange for the use of a tractor and plow and other equipment George would do some work for Whitman. George plowed up about 6 or 8 acres and planted half of it with potatoes and half of it with pickles. The soil was not that good on the farm and George didn't get as large a crop as he planned on. He did get enough potatoes to see the family through the winter but didn't have very much left over to sell like he thought he would. He did better with the pickles and sold them to the pickle factory in Fountain. That was the only bright spot in his attempt at farming. George Smith had a twenty-acre field he wanted seeded with clover for hay. The best way to get clover seeded was to plant the clover seed with oats then after you harvested the oats the first year the next year you would have clover for hay. So George made an agreement with him. George would buy the clover and oat seeds and plant them. He would then harvest the oats and sell them and George Smith would have his clover. Well, the soil on that field wasn't very good either and George lost his shirt on the deal, as well as his socks, his shoes, his pants and everything else. He didn't even harvest as many bushels of oats as he planted. I think that for every bushel of oats he planted he only got about three-quarters of a bushel in return. At least George Smith got his clover.

  When George wasn't busy hoeing, weeding and picking pickles on his own farm he found work with other farmers around town. He worked in the onion fields weeding and harvesting onions. During haying season he helped other farmers with bailing and hauling hay. During thrashing season he worked in the fields loading wagons or what ever work he could find. He picked berries, cherries and other fruit when they were in season. That fall he got a job at Daly's farm canning apples, he would set on a stool and feed the apples, one at a time into the apple peeler. He peeled a lot of apples that fall. It was an assembly line set up. George would peel the apples then they went on to a conveyer belt where the women would slice and core the apples, then they were washed and put into large cans and then into the freezer.

The winter of 1949 to spring 1950, George headed for the woods. After deer season of course. Phil Sterling had a contract to supply bolts to the paper mill in Manistee. So George got himself a Swede saw or bow saw as some people call it now and an axe and went to work for him. George would get assigned an area to cut and he was pretty much on his own. He got paid by the cord, so what he made depended on how hard he worked. It was all poplar trees that they were cutting. George would cut down the trees, trim them and cut the bolts into eight-foot lengths and pile them in stacks four feet high and eight feet wide. A cord of wood is four feet high, four feet wide and eight feet long. He had to clear or cut a road into each stack so the trucks could get in to pick them up the following spring or summer. Some days when he was working in a stand of trees where the trees were close together he would do pretty good. Other days when the trees were more scattered or if he had to spend a lot of time clearing out a road to the bolts he didn't make so much. How much he made that winter I don't know because he didn't get paid until the bolts were delivered to the paper mill the following summer. By then George was in the Navy so he assigned his earnings to Grandma to pay for his room and board that winter. I hope she got paid, but knowing Phil Sterling I am sure that she did.

It was hard work but George didn't mind; he was use to hard work and it was the only work available that winter.

One morning that winter George got up to go to work and it was snowing and quite windy. So George decided not to go to work since he was only being paid for the amount of wood he cut and not by the hour. Oscar was there because he had been laid off at the Brunswick in Muskegon. So after breakfast when George didn't get ready to go to work Oscar ask him "Aren't you going to work today?" George replied "No, maybe later if it clears up." Oscar said, "Well I see that you are not going to set the world on fire." Then Grandpa said, "I am not worried about George setting the world on fire, I am more worried that the world will burn up and George won't even know it." Cleo was there and she lit into both of them and told them to stop picking on George.

The spring of 1950 George heard that the Norge in Muskegon was hiring so he headed back down to Muskegon and got a job at the Norge. He was working the night shift from midnight to 7AM. You worked seven hours and got paid for eight as a bonus for working the night shift. He operated the punch press and the power shears cutting and forming the metal parts. The hardest part was getting used to coming home from work, eating breakfast and going to bed. It was hard getting to sleep when the sun was shining. Some days George would sleep for three or four hours then get up and spend the afternoon running around then go back to bed about 8 PM and catch a couple of hours sleep before it was time to go to work. Other days he would sleep most of the day and spend the evening running around until it was time to go to work. That job only lasted about a month, then he was laid off again.

George didn't want to go back to farming since he hadn't done very well the summer before. So he tried all the factories in Muskegon and Grand Rapids and none of them were hiring. Most of them were laying off and cutting back so there just weren't any jobs available. It looked like George was running out of options and he wasn't sure what he would do. So he went down to the Navy recruiting office and enlisted in the Navy. He thought maybe he could learn enough about the operation of a ship and maybe get some training as a coxswain mate or a fireman and come back after four years and get a job on the car ferries out of Ludington and have a career sailing Lake Michigan. That wasn't the way things turned out but it kind of what he had in mind when he enlisted.

On June 20, 1950 George was put on a bus to Chicago by the Navy recruiter in Muskegon. Later that day he was sworn into the Navy in Chicago and shipped off to Great Lakes Naval Training Center to start a new career and a new chapter in his life. He had no idea what the next four years would hold for him and how his life would be changed. He only knew he would have a place to sleep and three meals a days for a least four years.

Chapter Three
Deer Hunting in Michigan

The Davison's were all hunters so it was only natural that George would become a hunter too. When Grandpa was young he use to supplement his income by selling the meat and fur and hides of the game he killed. One day George and Grandpa were talking about hunting and Grandpa said, "When I was young I used to hunt for money." Grandma overheard him and she said, "Well, I still have to." When they were on the farm Grandpa always had a pack of hunting hounds for rabbits, fox, and coon. One day he was talking about an old hound he called Red. Red was a good rabbit dog but he had one weakness. When you jumped a rabbit the rabbit would usually run in a circle and come back close to the place where he was first jumped. The hunters would spread out near the spot where the rabbit was jumped and wait for the dogs to chase the rabbit back to them. Well, old Red got smart and figured out what was going on. While the rest of the pack was chasing the rabbit he would cut across and wait for the rabbit and catch it before it got back to the hunters. One of the hunters with Grandpa one day got so upset because he never got to shoot a rabbit that he said he was going to shoot that damn dog.

The Davison's boys were all good hunters and most of them were good shots, except George he was just lucky. Oscar would out shoot them all when they were shooting at targets. Vern was the best shot when it came to shooting at running or flying game. One day

George said he thought the sights on his rifle needed adjusting. Vern said let me see, he took George's rifle and told George to throw a can in the air. George threw the can up and Vern hit it twice before it hit the ground. Vern handed the rifle back to George and said "There is nothing wrong with your sights". Nelt was the best hunter of the bunch. He always seem to know where the deer would be and where they would be going once they were jumped. He could spot a deer far off before anyone else could and move into position to be able shoot when it came into range. He was the only one that would fill his tag every year, usually on the first day of the season, and then help the rest get their deer.

    Starting in 1944, after the war, the Davison's would set up camp on the south edge of the Bear Swamp near Millerton. They would set up two tents. Whitman made two stoves out of old oil drums that they would use for cooking and heating the tents. You would get up in the morning and it would be cold as all get out in the tents but once you got the fire going the tents would warm up fast. Then you would have to open the flaps on the tents because it would get to hot in there. There was a small creek flowing across the road just west of the camp. Some years when it was real wet you couldn't cross the creek with a car. When that happen some one would drive their car in from the other side so we would have cars on both sides of the creek. We would hunt in the swamp between our camp and the Sable River and in the plains and woods south of camp. Sometimes we would put a boat in the Sable River and float it down the river to a spot just north of our camp. Then we could cross the river to hunt. We would leave it there until deer season was over then float it on down to the Pole Bridge. We camped there four years through 1947. After that we hunted from Oscar's cottage at Ford Lake, but we still returned to the same area to hunt just had to drive a little further was all. One night when we were at Oscar's cottage we heard what sounded like a bobcat howling just outside. Everyone grabbed a flashlight and went out side and started shinning the lights into the trees to see if they could find the bobcat. Well, the old bobcat figured he better get out of there so he jumped down out of the tree and hit the ground running about 5 feet from where George was standing. Too darn close for comfort.

The Davison boys liked their booze as well as anyone but they had one unwritten rule in deer camp. Guns and alcohol don't mix. No one took a bottle in the field when they went hunting and they didn't break out the bottle at the end of the day until everyone was back in camp and the guns were all unloaded and put away.

George hunted six years in Michigan before he went in to the Navy. With a lot of luck and some help from Vern and Nelson he was able to fill his tag five of the six years that he hunted. The first year wasn't one of the lucky years for him. One day he was setting on a stand on a poplar knoll that ran down in to the swamp just about to the river. It wasn't very high but it divided the swamp with water on both sides of the knoll. A big tree had blown over and George was sitting on the trunk of the tree with the roots in front of him making a perfect blind. He could see out over and around the roots but was well hidden himself. A herd of does came by within ten or fifteen yards from where George was sitting. A few minutes later George saw the buck sneaking along behind the does. The buck was staying in the thicker brush and didn't come out in the open like the does did. But he kept coming closer. When he was about twenty yards from George and moving away, George decided that was as close as he was going to get. The buck was broadside to George but still in the thick brush, so George took his first shot at a deer. George was hunting with a single barrel 20-gauge shotgun with slugs, so he only had one shot. When George shot, the buck whirled and went right back the way he came. By the time George could reload the buck was out of sight. George checked the area where the buck was for blood and tracked it until it went in to the water in the swamp but couldn't find any sign of blood or that he had hit the buck. How anyone could miss a deer standing broadside to them only about twenty yards away I don't know but George did. He said that his bullet must have hit a branch in the thick brush and ricocheted away. Anyway it was the first, but not the last deer that George would shoot at and miss.

    The next year, 1945, George got his first buck. Okay, Vern had to shoot it for him but he counted it as his first buck. Don't try to tell him different, it was his first buck. George and Vern were standing on an old railroad grade and saw a herd of deer cross the grade about a quarter of a mile from them. A little later another deer came up to the edge of the grade and stopped. Vern said "That is a buck," so George pulled up his old 20-gauge and shot. The deer took one leap across the grade and then Vern shot. Then Vern turned to George and asked, "What were you shooting at?" George replied, "Well, you said it was a buck." Vern laughed and said

"Okay, but your shotgun won't shoot that far, it was way out of your range." There had been a light snow the night before and as they were walking down the grade to where the deer had crossed they saw a fresh groove plowed in the snow. Vern said to George "That is where your slug ended up." It was about half way to where the deer was so George was way short on that shot. When they got to where the deer had crossed there was fresh blood every where and a few feet off the grade they found a nice spike horn buck. I told you that Vern was the best shot at a moving target. If that deer had been standing still Vern probably would have missed it. Vern told George that he could have it and he showed George how to clean it out and what to do, but he made George do it. Since it was a spike horn buck George had to put his tag in the deer's ear. When George went to slice a hole in the ear to put the tag he was so excited he sliced his index finger on his left hand and still has a scar to prove it.

The next year, 1946, George ran down his first deer; anyway, that is what Vern and Nelson both said. They said that George didn't have to shoot a deer. He just chased it and ran after it until it dropped. That is just about what happened but George did have to shoot at it a couple of times before it dropped. Even though he missed the first shot and the deer was too tired to run anymore when George shot the second time.

    George and his cousin Jimmy were hunting in the same area that George had gotten his deer the year before. They were working their way through the woods about forty yards apart when this big buck jumped up and ran past George back the way they had just come. George got off one shot with his old single shot 20-gauge. There was good tracking snow and when George went over to where the deer had went by he found blood, so he hollered at Jimmy and told him he had hit the buck. They both started tracking it. They tracked it a little ways and found that it had fallen down and then gotten back up and took off again. That got the old adrenaline flowing and they started moving faster. A little further on they found where it had fallen and got back up again. The buck circled around them and started going back in the other direction. It kept falling and getting back up and they knew they were getting closer. Then the buck jumped up right in front of them and George got another shot and the buck went down. George yelled, "I got him" and ran up to the deer and picked up his head by the horns. Just then, the buck tried to get up on his front legs, so George had to shoot him again in the head. It was a nice eight point buck with four even spaced points on each side. Vern and Nelson were both hunting in the same area. They both said they heard George yell when he first shot at the deer and that it was only about ten minutes later and a mile away when they heard George yell again that he had gotten the deer. That is why they said that George ran the deer to death instead of shooting him. Actually it was only about a half a mile and more like twenty or thirty minutes but George never lived it down. When they got the deer back to camp and started examining it closer they determined that George had missed it the first time he shot at it. The wound that was bleeding and caused the deer to fall so often was in the right front shoulder and when the deer went past George he was shooting at the left side of the deer. So George couldn't have caused that wound. Someone must have shot it the day before and never found it. The second time George shot at it the deer was going straight away from him and George hit it right in the back and the bullet traveled right up the deer's back right beside the spine and lodged in his neck. That is the shot that brought the deer down.

  The next year, 1947, George started out to the same area he'd gotten his first two deer. There was good tracking snow and on the way there he came across what looked like a fresh track with some blood. There wasn't a lot of blood but enough so George knew that the deer had been shot and it looked like it was walking on just three legs. George figured it must be a leg wound but couldn't tell how serious. George tracked it for a while then a deer jumped up off to his left. George couldn't see any horns and the tracks he was following were going off to the right. So he figured it must be a doe. He let it go and kept following the tracks and they doubled back around right to where that deer had been laying. Now George was confused, was he tracking a doe someone shot at the day before or was it a buck? George didn't see the horns when it jumped up in front of him. Because it was going in the direction that George was planning to hunt, he decided to stay with it and see if he could get a better look at the deer. After tracking the deer for about another mile, George came upon a small cluster of pine trees and the tracks went right through them. Just as George was about to step out of the pines he saw the deer laying in a clearing about twenty yards in front of him. The deer was laying there looking back at him and George still couldn't see any horns. Then the deer turned his head and George saw a horn. That year George had a double barrel shotgun with a slug in one barrel and buckshot in the other barrel. So George gave him a load of buckshot in the head. The buck had one spike horn about six inches long on one side, the other side had been broken off and there was only a knob on that side. That is why George couldn't see any horns when he first saw the deer. So there was another deer that George was accused of running to death before he shot him. George was a long way from camp but he found a road and a car that he knew who it belonged to so he dragged his deer up there and waited for them to come back and give him a ride back to camp.

Just north and east of camp there was an area they called the Cedar Swamp. It covered an area not more than a quarter of a mile wide and about three-quarters of a mile long. Not too many people hunted in there because it was so thick and if you did jump a deer you didn't have much of a chance of getting a shot at it. George was about to find out. The best way to hunt that area was to get a group of hunters and have them stationed along the edge and then have one or two hunters go into the cedars and try to flush the deer out. One afternoon it was snowing quite hard and the wind was blowing. So George decided it might be a good time to hunt in the cedar swamp away from the wind and snow. There were a few trails winding through the swamp but most of it was just thick cedar trees and you couldn't see very far in any direction. George would walk around until he could find a place where he could see for a little ways then he would stand and wait. Then he would move on to another location. At one of his stops he was just watching and listening and he thought he heard something. He looked over in that direction but at first he couldn't see anything. Then he saw what looked like a deer's eye, and then he saw its nose and part of its head about fifteen or twenty feet away. It was just standing there and not moving. The deer knew someone or something was there but didn't know just where George was. After what seemed like a long time but was probably only a few seconds, the deer whirled and was gone in the blink of an eye. When the deer turned, George could see that it had a nice set of horns but that is all he could see. He never saw the rest of the deer and, of course, he was not able to get a shot at it. After wandering around in there most of the afternoon, George came upon another set of boot tracks so he decided that there must be another hunter in there too. George followed the tracks for a little ways then thought that those tracks looked kind of familiar. He put his foot down beside one of the boot prints and then looked at the two prints and sure enough they were identical. He had walked around in a circle and was following his own tracks. George knew that the river was to the north and that the road ran along the south side of the cedar swamp. He got out his compass and took a reading, he knew he had to go south. When he looked to the south he saw a solid wall of cedar trees with snow on the branches hanging all the way to the ground. He knew he was going to have to go through them to get out. So he lowered his head and plowed and clawed his way through. He only went about ten feet and found himself out of the cedars and just a short distant from the road. Lesson number one: never go into the woods without your compass. Lesson number two: no matter how many deer you see in the cedar swamp you will never get a shot at one.

    Early one morning George made his way down into the swamp just north of camp. He found himself a good place to sit right on the edge of the cedar swamp looking out towards the hardwood swamp. He had just gotten settled when he saw a herd of deer moving through the hardwoods towards the cedars. A few minutes latter another lone deer came along behind them. George was sure it was a buck but it was just getting light and there wasn't enough light to see if the deer had horns or not. So George had to let it go. Later that morning George was sitting there with his back to a big tree and he heard a hunter coming up behind him. There was some ice on the water in the swamp and every step the hunter took you could hear him breaking through the ice. George said to himself "Well, he is going to scare all the deer away for awhile." So George set his gun down resting against the tree and got up and lit a cigarette. He heard the hunter stop just behind him so George stepped out from behind the tree so the hunter would be sure to see him. I don't know who was the most surprised George or the big buck he was face-to-face with about fifteen yards away. Before George could even make a move for his gun the buck whirled and disappeared back into the swamp. Lesson number three: deer don't always sneak around the woods without being heard. They can make just as much noise as a man does if the conditions are right.

  1948, one morning George and Nelson were going to hunt together. They had just parked their car at the end of the old railroad grade. In the same area George had gotten his first three deer. As they were getting ready to start out they saw a deer cross the grade. They both thought it was a buck but it was moving to fast for them to tell for sure or get a shot at it. Nelson told George that the deer would probably head for a small marsh just south of where they were. He told George to go down there by the end of the marsh and find a place where he could cover the area and he would go down to where the deer had crossed and track it through. George did what Nelson told him and found a good stand on top of a big pine stump about four feet high. The buck did just what Nelson said it would do. The buck was coming right at George, when George saw it he started to raise his rifle and the buck saw George. The buck stopped and looked at George and George stood real still looking at the buck. They both stood there staring at each other for a few seconds then the buck whirled and made a big jump to get out of there. George brought his rifle up and shot just as the buck was in the middle of his jump. The buck went crashing down in a heap and never finished his jump. George hit him right behind the shoulder and the bullet came out his neck. That was the first year George hunted with his old 30-40 Winchester that his dad had gave him.

    The next year, 1949, they were staying at Oscar's cottage at Ford Lake. It was getting near the end of deer season and George hadn't gotten his deer yet. It had been raining the day before and most of the night and had melted all the snow. The rest of them didn't feel like going hunting that day so George was going to go by himself. Then Nelson said he would go with him. They drove up to an area that they called the Still Swamp, don't know why they called it that I guess someone must have had a still near there during Probation. Nelson helped George find a good spot to sit then he went off to scout around and find a spot for himself. George sat there about an hour when a herd of does came by and sure enough there was a buck following along behind them. George had a good broad side shot at the buck at about thirty yards. George got a little nervous and instead of shooting him in the front shoulder or the chest area. He hit him to far back and gut shot him. The buck took off and George emptied his gun at him. George knew he hit him with the first shot because he saw the buck buckle. Sure enough he found blood and was able to track him about one hundred yards when he jumped him again. Again George emptied his gun at him without hitting anything. Nelson heard George shooting but wasn't sure it was George. He said the shots were too fast for a lever action rifle and thought it was some one with an automatic rifle. He came over to check on George and saw the buck running across the field but couldn't get a shot at him. When George told him what had happened Nelson said the buck would probably head for the river. So instead of trying to track the buck they both headed for the river. I told you before that Nelson was the best hunter of the bunch and always seemed to know where the deer would go. He was right again. They found a set of tracks and blood right by the river where Nelson said the buck would go. The buck had crossed the river so George found a place to cross the river and found the tracks going down stream from where they were. Nelson told George to give him a few minutes to try and get ahead of the deer and then start tracking him. George waited until Nelson was in place then started tracking the buck. He only went about fifty yards and he saw the buck laying in the grass about twenty feet ahead of him. George tried to shoot him in the head but shot off his lower jaw instead. The buck jumped up and ran across the river and George emptied his gun at him again. The buck started down river toward Nelson. Nelson saw it and got a couple of shots at it and the buck turned and came right back to where George was and stopped right across the river from George. George yelled at Nelson and said "The buck is standing right across the river from me". Nelson said, "Shoot it" George, replied "I can't, I am out of shells." George had fired fifteen shots at that deer and only hit it twice and it was still going. The deer went on up the river. George waited until Nelson got there and told him where the deer had gone.

Nelson went looking for the deer while George found a place to cross the river again. George got across the river and started upstream to where Nelson was when he heard Nelson yell. "Here is you buck, George, dead." George took a couple of steps and then he heard Nelson shoot twice. He looked up and saw the deer coming right at him. The buck was trapped between Nelson and George but George was out of ammunition. The buck turned away from the river and stopped a little ways out in the trees and Nelson was able to bring him down with another shot. But he wasn't ready to give up yet. When they got over to him, the buck tried to get up and Nelson had to slit it's throat with his hunting knife. The buck had a nice set of horns but it was the skinniest and one of the toughest deer we ever ate. I guess they ran all the fat off him chasing around the woods all day.

That was the last deer George shot in Michigan. He went into the Navy the following summer and it would be thirty years before he got to go hunting in Michigan again, ten years before he got to go deer hunting again and that was in Arizona.

I don't remember for sure what year it was but George was still in high school so it must have been either 1946 or 1947. One of Vern's friends and his two sons came up from Grand Rapids to go hunting with us on the last day of the season, which was a Sunday. Late in the afternoon he shot a deer but didn't know if it was a buck or a doe. He sent one of his son's and George to check it out. It was a doe so they got out of there fast. The next day when George got home from school Whitman was at Grandma's and he asked George if he thought he could find the doe the guy had shot the day before in the dark. George said he thought he could. They didn't want to see the meat go to waste. So after supper George and Whitman drove up to the wood. The deer wasn't to far from the road and they were able to find it right away. Some one else had found it and had started to clean it out but some one must have scared them away because the job was only half done. George and Whitman finished cleaning it out and put it in the back of Whitman's truck and he took it out to his farm and hung it up in the barn. So he had venison for the winter.

Chapter Four
The Navy Years

ODE TO A SAILOR
Author Unknown

In the peacetime he's a hoodlum, a drunken, lazy gob.
He's really in the Navy, 'cause he couldn't find a job.
He's the lowest sort of vermin, the specimen of an ass.
He can't get any lower, cause he's the lowest class.
He's the blackest of the vandals, he's rotten, vulgar, vile
He must have learned his manners, from the inmates of his style.
He's a danger to the city, the very lowest class.
In peacetime he's a villain, a drunken, rowdy ass.
He's always chasing women. The loose ones, if you please.
He's just about as welcome, as a whispered named disease.
He's the salesman of the stories, (the Farmers' Daughter Brand).
He's just above the canine; He shakes the devil's hand.
His mine is in the gutter, In a bottle is his heart.
He'll win the race to Hades, 'cause he's he got a six year start.
He's the famous snake of Hell, the wolf of Riding Hood.
He's the spider in the parlor, the boogey in the wood.
In peacetime there's a reason, on the ocean he must stay,
He needs the ocean water, to wash the filth away.

When peace slips out of vision, WAR holds it's gruesome way,
The horse has changed it's color, so here the cry today!!!
He's the nations' brave defender, He's strong and brave and bold.
He's out to fight our battles, Our lives to save, we're told.
He's far from home and mother, so lonely, don't we know.
The very least that we can do, is join the USO.
Invite him out to dinner; give him a glass of beer
He needs our best devotion, His loyal heart to cheer.

*It's quite a different story, now there's a need for you.
He's not the painted devil, My sons in the Navy too.
He's the man behind the gun, the toast in all the bars.
He doesn't go to movies; he 's living with the stars.
He's the apple of the orchard, Until the war is done,
He's a darn important fellow, until the war is won.
He's the fashion of the season, but when there's peace once more,
He'll be the slimy bastard that he was before the war.*

June 20, 1950, George left Muskegon and went down to Chicago to be sworn into the Navy. He was sent to Great Lakes Naval Training Center just north of Chicago for boot camp. He had only been in boot camp 5 days when the Korean War broke out on June 25, 1950. He was glad he was in the Navy because other wise he would have been drafted into the army at that time.

While George was in boot camp the Navy was looking for a few good men to fill up the fall classes at the Naval Academy at Annapolis. They were giving all the recruits in boot camps who were interested, a chance to take the test, so George decided to take it. He passed the written test and then went for his physical. The minimum height requirement was five feet, six inches. Because they shaved George's head when he arrived at boot camp he came up short at five feet, five and three-quarters inches. They said they might be able to wave that requirement if he did real well on the last part of the test. The last part was an interview with five high ranking Naval Officers. When George walked into the room and saw those officers setting there in their dress blues, with more gold on their uniforms than in Fort Knox, he froze. He was as nervous as a cat on a hot tin roof. George stammered and stuttered his way through the interview and when he walked out of that room he knew that he had blown any chance he had of going to the Naval Academy and becoming an admiral.

    George was about half way through boot camp when his mother became sick and had to go to the hospital. She wasn't expected to live so George was given a week's furlough to go home and be with her. When George got back to boot camp they assigned him to a different company, because he had missed a week of training with his original company. He had to make new friends and kind of start over again.

    When George joined the Navy he did well on his written test and was guaranteed a school if he so desired. So when he finished boot camp George put in for Aviation Electronics School. In September of 1950 George was sent to Memphis Tenn. For eight weeks of Aircraft Fundamental school and then was to continue on with his Aviation Electronics school for twenty-eight weeks. George had just started his Electronics school when one morning he woke up with a sore throat, some one convinced him to go to sick bay. While he was sitting on a bench in sick bay waiting for a doctor he went to sleep and woke up in the hospital with a bad case of tonsillitis and a temperature close to one hundred and four degrees. Penicillin was a fairly new drug at that time and the only way to administer it then was with a shot. So every four hours they would come by and roll George over and stick a needle in his behind. By the time they got his temperature down and he began feeling better, his butt felt like it had been used for a pincushion. I can only imagine what it must have looked like. George spent Thanksgiving in the hospital. They served a complete Thanksgiving dinner with turkey and all the trimmings but George didn't enjoy it very much because he was so sick. George found out that it was easier to get into the Navy hospital that it was to get out. They wouldn't release him until they were sure he would be able to return to full active duty. They couldn't send him back to the barracks to recuperate so they kept him in the hospital until he was completely well. He spent a month in the hospital before he was allowed to return to school. After George got to feeling better they assigned him to light kitchen duty in the ward he was in. When his work was done he would sit around in the kitchen drinking juice which they kept in the refrigerator. The day George was to be released from the hospital he broke out in a bad rash that covered most of his body so they kept him for another week. They though the rash was caused by all the citrus juice he had been drinking.

In December George was finally released from the hospital and returned to his school. Because he had missed a month of school, once again, George was reassigned to a new class and had to start over again just like he had to do in boot camp.

The spring of 1951 Oscar brought Grandma and the kids down to Memphis to spend a weekend with George. He was glad to see them. Retta also came down to Memphis one weekend to spend some time with George.

George finished Aviation Electronics school in July 1951 and was given a short leave to go home before he had to report for duty at North Island Navel Air Station in San Diego. In San Diego it was back to school for four weeks of Basic Radar Operation before he was assigned to Squadron VS 871 stationed at Los Alamitos Naval Air Station just out side of Long Beach, California. While he was in San Diego, George decided he needed a car so he put a deposit down on a 1938 Studerbaker. He had Grandma send him his bonds he was having withheld from his pay. Before the bonds got there and George was able to pick up his car one of the salesmen took it out and wrecked it. They gave George a 1941 Plymouth coupe in place of the Studerbaker for the same price. One weekend George and a couple of his buddies went up to Los Angeles, George was going to visit his Aunt Glee and Uncle Al.

The brakes went out when they were in Long Beach and George rear ended another car and smashed up the front end and the radiator. They were only about ten miles from Glee's and Al's so Al came down and towed the car to their place. So George was without a car for awhile. Al helped George get a new radiator and repair most of the damage to the front end but it was about a month before George was back on the road again. By that time he was stationed at Los Alamitos.

The spring of 1952, George was granted a two-week leave, so he packed up the Plymouth and headed for Michigan. George left Los Alamitos about 6:00 one Friday night and 72 hours later he pulled into Muskegon. The first night he drove from LA to Flagstaff Arizona, and that day he drove from Flagstaff to Tucumcari, New Mexico. He wasted a couple of hours in Albuquerque, New Mexico when the brakes on his car started to fade. He stopped at a couple of garages before he found one that told him his problem was that the brakes were to tight and causing air in the brake lines when they got warmed up. They loosened up the brakes and bled the air out of the lines and he didn't have any more trouble the rest of the trip. That night he slept in the car at Tucumcari and got an early start the next morning. The second night he got a room at a hotel in the southeast corner of the state of Kansas on old Route 66. It was too cold to sleep in the car. He was going to spend the next night some where in northern Indiana or southern Michigan, but when he stopped for gas late that afternoon in Indiana they had a big sign that gave the mileage's to different city's from that point. When George saw how close he was to Muskegon he decided to go for it with out spending another night on the road. When he got out of the car in Muskegon he could hardly stand up and walk he was so tired. 72 hours from LA to Muskegon and there were no freeways back then just old Route 66. He hadn't told anyone he was coming so they were all surprised when he walked in the door at Clayton's.

George didn't rush so much on his way back to LA. He took his time and enjoyed a little of the scenery. He spent one night in Gallup, N.M. and the next morning he drove to the Painted Desert. He got there a little after sunrise and the Painted Desert was beautiful that time of the morning. George has been back to the Painted Desert a couple of times since but he has never seen the colors as bright and as pretty as they were that morning. That was before the Painted Desert became a National Park. All you had to do was pull off the highway and drive along the edge of the cliffs overlooking the desert on a dirt road. You could stop anywhere along the edge of the cliffs and take pictures, which George did. George left there and headed for the Petrified Forest. He spent a couple of hours there and then on to Flagstaff and to the Grand Canyon. George entered the Grand Canyon from the East End and saw it grow deeper and wider as he traveled the length of the park. George had just purchased a 35mm camera before his trip so he took lots of pictures. He still has the slides he took that day of the Painted Desert, The Petrified Forest and the Grand Canyon and likes to compare them to ones he took later. The parks have all changed over the years. George spent that night in Williams and the next day drove on to Los. Angeles and back to the base.

George started having problems with the Plymouth after he got back from Michigan so he traded it in and got a 1948 Dodge sedan. Later that summer he got another short leave and went up to Northern California and spent a week with his cousins Nancy, Charles, Patty, and John Bell, who lived near Santa Rosa just north of San Francisco. Their mother ran a small store in one of the resort communities on the Russian River. George had a ball that week, swimming in the river during the day, dancing every night at the resort and hanging out in the store with his cousins and the family.

When George was at Los Alamitos there wasn't a Disneyland to go to, it opened in 1956. If Disneyland had been there at that time it would have been about six miles off the East End of the main runway right in our flight path. Knotts Berry Farm was open and only about four miles from the base. At that time it was a small Western Theme Park with free admission. George would go there and spend an afternoon wandering around taking in the sights and enjoying the shows they put on. You had to pay for the rides and to get in to some of the shows but you could spend a day there without spending a lot of money. They had a restaurant and the food was good; a whole lot better than Navy chow. The first time George went there, he went with Glee and Al. As they were walking around they came to an old jail that had a dummy locked up inside. When George looked inside the dummy called him by name and started talking to him. George couldn't figure out how he knew who he was. Later he found out that Al had gone around back of the jail and gave some information to a man back there who had a mike and speaker and that is who was talking to George. Glee and Al lived in Redondo Beach only about twenty miles from the base so George would go there quite often. Friday nights Glee and Al use to do their grocery shopping and then stop at a restaurant for supper, sometime George would meet them at the restaurant. George spent a lot of weekends with them. Sheila was about four years old and George use to tease her and called her a "Nincompoop." She would get so upset and stomp her foot and say, "Don't call me that!" I don't think she even knew what it meant but she didn't like the sound of it.

  George's favorite hang out, while he was at Los Alamitos, was the Long Beach Pier. It was an amusement park on the waterfront with game booths and rides and a ballroom. Les Brown and His Band of Renown played there on weekends and that is where you would find George just about every Saturday night, sometime on Friday and Sunday too. The band had a young girl who sang with them named J.P. Morgan. She was as cute as could be and could she ever sing. George especially liked to hear her sing "I'm LITTLE, BUT I'm LOUD;" boy could she belt that out and make the rafters ring. George met a lot of girls there but he never dated any of them. George also went dancing a couple of time at the Santa Monica Pier and Ballroom when Lawrence Welk and his band were there, but he didn't like it as much as he did in Long Beach.

The squadron had a softball team and George played on it. They played in a city league off the base. One night George was catching and he got hit on the little finger of his right hand by a foul tip. It bent the tip of his finger straight back and sure hurt. He went to sickbay when he got back to the base and they straighten the finger out but it never healed properly. George still can't bend the knuckle of that finger.

Sky Room of the Wilton Hotel

In September, 1952, one of George's buddies, Dick Mabrey, had a date with a nurse. Dick had a motorcycle but didn't want to make her ride on the back end of the motorcycle. So he asked George if he could borrow his car. Well, George wasn't about to lend his car to anyone so he said no. Dick then asked his date, Lila if she could get one of the other nurses to go on a blind date with George and they would go on a double date. She talked Mary Lira into going with them. So on Saturday night, September 20, 1952 George and Dick drove over to Compton Sanitarium and picked up the girls. Mary and Lila were both working and going to school at the Sanitarium studying Psychiatry Nursing. There wasn't any place in Arizona to study Psychiatry Nursing at that time. They went to the Sky Room of the Wilton Hotel in downtown Long Beach for dinner and an evening of dancing. George couldn't even remember Mary's last name and he didn't get her phone number. He had to ask Dick a couple of days later after they got back to the base for them. George finally worked up enough nerve to call Mary and ask her to go to the drive-in movies with him. They went to see Son of Paleface, a movie they had both seen before but didn't want the other one to know they had seen it. The next month was a whirlwind courtship, a day at the beach, a day at the amusement park on the pier, a day driving around to see some of the sights and just being together. One Sunday evening they drove up to San Pedro Point to watch the sun set. After the sun went down the fog rolled in and George got lost on the way home. The fog was so thick you couldn't see very far and George had not been in that part of town before. They finally got back to an area that George recognized and got home safe. George was scared but he never told Mary they were lost. October 27, 1952 George and his squadron were deployed to the South Pacific. He didn't know if he would ever see Mary again but he started writing to her and she wrote to him. When George got back from overseas the end of February 1953 he went to

Arizona to see Mary and meet her family. He proposed to her and she said yes. For the next year George would make the drive from Los Alamitos to Phoenix about once a month. Dick Mabrey's parents lived in Glendale so he would come with George sometimes. But most of the time George made the trip by himself.

After Mary passed away George was going through some of her papers and he found some notes she had left and the following is her account of what happened in her words. She must have had some pictures to go with this but George couldn't find them.

Mary and George

Personal shower given on June 7, 1954 7P.M. By friends Katie Hausley, Karye Muciste, Arlene Gordon, Beverly Frances, Reta Maloney, Vickie Hopkins, Eleanor Dark, Marrgie Eggers, Brenda North.

Mary and George met on September 20, 1952 Saturday 8 P.M. They met in Long Beach California. George was in the Navy stationed there at Los Alamitos Navy Air Base. Mary was going to school in Compton.

This is where George and Mary went on their first date, on September 20, 1952. Saturday night. This is the Wilton Hotel, George and Mary went dancing at the Sky Room at this hotel. It was a beautiful night with a bright moon and a million stars and you could see the ocean below. It was beautiful. This is the building where George and Mary met. This is George and he and Mary went to the beach on their third date.

George and Mary went to the movies on their second date, Thursday September 26, 1952. They saw "Son of Paleface."

September 29. It was a beautiful Sunday they went to Long Beach. It was a wonderful day for both of them. After that they went to San Pedro Hills to watch the setting of the sun. This is the Way Fares Chapel, it is all made of glass and is in San Pedro. George and Mary went to see it. This is the entrance of the LA Museum where George took Mary on their last date before he was shipped overseas. It was on a Sunday October 25, 1952

George went overseas on October 27, 1952. It was a Tuesday. He sailed at 1 p.m. on the Bataan ship.

Mary came home on November 8, 1952.

George and Mary wrote to each other every day while he was gone. For Christmas George sent Mary a telegraph from Okinawa wishing her a Merry Christmas. That was the best present Mary got for Christmas that year

George came home from overseas on February 27, 1953. He sent Mary a telegram from Hawaii telling her when he would reach the States. He docked in San Diego and telephoned Mary from there. He came to see her on March 3, 1953 and he brought Mary oodles of gifts from overseas. A yellow silk robe, a blue silk scarf, two more scarves, a beautiful black jewelry box, a cross with chain.

George proposed marriage to Mary March 6, 1953 and Mary said yes. George was home ten days and then he went back to the naval base. He came to see Mary again on April 6. Mary got her engagement ring that day. It was the most beautiful ring ever. Its yellow gold with a big diamond and two heart shaped diamond chips on each side. She also got his wedding ring to match her engagement ring. But no plans are set for the wedding. George went back to the base and all that summer they wrote each other every day.

George was able to come and see Mary at least once a month. In September 17, 1953 he came home on leave for two weeks and they planed the wedding for June, 1954. George was home again for Christmas and they set the wedding for June 20, 1954. So the wedding plans began to roll. Then it was April 1954 and George came home discharged from the service, and final wedding arrangements were made.

George and Mary were married on June 20, 1954 and they had the most beautiful wedding ever. They went away for a few days *and came back and got ready for their honeymoon trip to the east, George's home.*

After Mary accepted George's proposal George knew Mary wanted to get married in the Catholic Church so when he got back to the base he went to see a priest in a small Catholic Church just off the base in Los Alamitos. They didn't have a Catholic chaplain at the base. The priest agreed to give George the instructions to become a Catholic and one of George's drinking buddies, Roger Davis agreed to sponsor him. George took the instructions and was baptized into the Catholic Church in the fall of 1953.

George and Mary use to kid about having met at an insane asylum. Those who knew Mary was a nurse thought George must have been a patient there. People who didn't know them would give them strange looks wondering which one was the crazy one. They both were. It was always good for a laugh.

When George was returning from the South Pacific they had a short stop in Hawaii. George and some of his drinking buddies found a small restaurant out away from the down town area where most of the sailors hung out. They got a pizza and had a couple of beers. After they finished the pizza they were sitting around drinking and George decided he had enough to drink and asked if they had any fresh milk. They didn't get fresh milk aboard ship. So George was sitting there drinking milk while the rest of them were drinking beer. One of them said, "You know that girl has really changed you George." Les Hardy spoke up and said, "No that girl didn't change George. I've known George longer that the rest of you and he always knew when he had enough to drink and was able to stop when he wanted to. That is one thing I've always admired about George." George and Les had been together since they were in school in Memphis.

One night George and Les Hardy and a couple of their buddies were in Santa Monica. Les had a girl friend there. They didn't get started back to the base until the wee hours of the morning. George was tired so he let Les drive. They were speeding down the Coast Highway, everything was closed and there wasn't any traffic on the road. When they got to Redondo Beach, Les blew through a red light and a cop pulled them over. He checked Les's license and asked him if it was his car. Les replied "No, it belongs to George." The cop then asked George for his license and registration. After checking them, he asked George why Les was driving. George told him it was because he was tired. Instead of giving them a ticket he just said, "Well, George you had better drive 'cause Les ain't doing so good." I guess he felt sorry for them because there were in the service. George drove the rest of the way back to the base without any more incidents.

When George was in San Diego he heard some of the sailors talking about going to the beach at La Hoya. George checked a map of the area and couldn't find La Hoya anywhere. The closest thing he could find was La Jolla. That is when he learned that the people in California didn't know how to spell any better that he did. Or that they didn't how to pronounce the English language. I am not sure what their problem was. George went down to Tijuana a couple of times to see the Jai Alai games, pronounced High Light. One night while he was there, he saw this gorgeous red head at the game. He is sure that it was Lucille Ball, "I Love Lucy." He wasn't able to get her autograph.

When George's grandson Rob was in college he had to do a report on the Korean War. He asked George to give him some information about what he remembered about his time in the Navy during the war. The following is a report that George wrote for Rob at that time.

The Korean War As I Remember It
By George E. Davison

I joined the Navy on June 20, 1950 and was in boot camp at Great Lakes when the Korean War broke out on June 25, 1950.

After boot camp I went to Memphis Naval Air Station in Memphis Tennessee, for training in Naval Aviation and Aviation Electronics. From there I went to San Diego North Island for advance electronics training, before being assigned to a squadron, VS-871, in the summer of 1951.

The squadron I was assigned to was a reserve squadron that had just been recalled to active duty. All the officers were reserve officers except for one regular Navy officer. They had all flown in World War II. About one-half to three-quarters of the enlisted men were also reserves. Some who had served in World War II. Some of the older ones were bitter about being recalled to active duty, because they had businesses, jobs, and family to leave behind. Most of them were from the San Francisco, Oakland California area. Regular Navy enlisted men, like myself, were assigned to the squadron to bring it up to full strength. We were stationed at Los Alamitos Naval Air Station just out side of Long Beach California.

Our squadron was an anti submarine squadron. Our mission was to track down and sink enemy submarines. Why they needed an anti submarine squadron in the Korean War I don't know. North Korea didn't have much of a Navy and no submarines that we knew of. I guess we were just being prepared in case China or Russia joined North Korea.

Our planes were all old TBM's, torpedo bombers, from World War II, that had been recondition and re-equipped for anti submarine duty. We flew in pairs, One plane was called the hunter and the other plane was called the killer. The hunter was loaded with long-range radar equipment and its job was to locate a submarine or target and direct the killer plane to the target. The killer plane would drop down low and fly just above the water so it couldn't be picked up on the submarine's radar, while the hunter plane would circle and direct the killer to the target.

I flew as a crewman in one of the killer planes. Beside the pilot we had a radar operator, a searchlight operator for night operations, who was also the torpedo man and I was an E.C.M. operator (electronics counter-measure). I had a lot of different electronic equipment to operate. One was a radar jammer, which was used to jam the enemy's radar so they couldn't track us.

TBM Torpedo Bomber
(Later converted to Sub Hunter)

Another was a scanner, which would scan the radio frequencies. When we picked up someone broadcasting on a frequency that we were not using, I would lock in on it and, with the aid of a direction finder, would pinpoint the direction it was coming from and we would try to home in on it. We couldn't tell how far away it was but we could get a fix on the direction and fly in on it as long as they kept broadcasting. If they went off the air we were out of luck.

Another important piece of equipment was our sonar receiver. If a submarine dived before we could attack, we would have to figure out which way it was going. We would drop sonar transmitters near where the sub was last seen. We would drop them in a pattern around the sub. Each transmitter was on a different frequency, then by switching back and forth to each channel, I could tell which way the sub was going. The sound would get louder or weaker as the sub got closer or further away from each transmitter. If the sub cut it's engines, sometimes I could hear people moving around in the sub to help fix it's location. But it was real hard. Other times the fish would start playing around the mike on the transmitter, they would really raise a rumpus but I could never understand what they were talking about. Fish do talk because I heard them.

Most of our training was done off the coast of California. We would chase fishing boats or our own ships and play war games with our own submarines. We made a couple of trips to El Centro so our pilots could practice night gunnery and bombing. El Centro was a god-forsaken place for a naval base, below sea level, nothing but sand and dust. It was hot and the wind blew all the time, blowing dust into everything. You had to shake the dust off your blankets before you went to bed and off your clothes when you got up in the morning. Thank goodness we were only there for two weeks at a time.

The longest flight I was on was a flight from Los Alamitos to Dallas, Texas, where we spent the night. The next day we flew to El Paso and spent the night and then back to Los Alamitos the next day with a stop in Phoenix. One of the pilots had a brother on the Phoenix police department he wanted to see, so he met us at the airport. When we landed in El Paso and were taxiing up to the tie down area, there were two planes tied down and our pilot decided to taxi between them. There was not much room, and someone working on one of the planes saw us coming and started waving his arms for us to stop. Just before we got to the planes our pilot folded our wings back and we shot between the two planes with room to spare. The guy on the ground stood there with his mouth open. I guess he had never seen a carrier plane that could fold its wings before. When we left El Paso we picked up two army men who needed a ride back to the Los Angeles area. So there were five of us in each plane. When we landed in Phoenix they sent a small truck out to pick us up and take us to the terminal. When we all got out of the plane the driver who had been sent to pick us up, wanted to know how many more were in the plane and where did we put everyone. He didn't expect to see that many people in a single engine plane.

We only had one fatality while I was with the squadron. He was an older pilot, much older that most of our pilots. They were practicing landing aboard a carrier at night and he took off from the carrier and started to circle to come around for a landing. He went in to a bank and never came out of it. He just kept banking until he crashed into the ocean. He must have lost his equilibrium. Since it was dark he couldn't tell the water from the sky. We never recovered his body.

One other close call that I can think of was when one of our pilots landed aboard the carrier and started to taxi to the front of the ship. Something happened that caused the plane to veer to the left and it went off the side of the carrier. Everyone on the flight deck went running over to the side, expecting to see the plane hit the water. But the pilot gave it full throttle and pulled up his landing gear as soon as he went over the side.

He got airborne just before he hit the water. He did skim the water but he made it. The TBM could maintain a flying speed of less than one hundred miles per hour. Most planes would not have been able to do that and it took a good pilot to do what he did.

I remember the first time I flew off a carrier. We were hooked up to the catapult, engine at full throttle and suddenly zoom we were flung forward like a rock out of a slingshot. The force pushed me back hard in my seat. Some of the knobs came off the radio equipment in front of me and hit me in the chest. Someone had left a screwdriver up under some of the equipment and it went flying by me and just missed me. After that I checked all the knobs on all the equipment to make sure they were all tight and checked under and around all the equipment to make sure there was nothing loose to go flying around.

I had a lot of faith in the pilots I flew with and was never worried or afraid. But there were a couple of times when maybe I should have been. Like the time we were coming in for a landing aboard the carrier and just as we were about to touch down we were given a wave off. The pilot gave it full throttle and pulled up to take us around for another try. The barrier on the flight deck was up and they said that our tail hook just missed catching the barrier as we went over it. If our tail hook had caught the barrier we would have nose-dived right into the flight deck. But we made it and came around for a successful landing. Another time we had been up most of the day chasing subs down by San Diego and were on our way back to the base. The pilot informed us we were running low on fuel and he was going to let one tank run dry before he switched tanks. A couple of minutes later the engine quit and then started up again when he switched tanks. Then he informed us that the tank had run dry and the gauge showed it was still a quarter full. So we didn't have as much fuel as he thought and it was going to be close. He got permission to land first and to come straight in with out circling like we would normally do. We landed OK and just turned off the runway onto the taxi strip when the plane stopped, out of gas. We had to be towed back to the tie down area.

    We received orders to go over seas in September of 1952. We boarded the aircraft carrier Bataan in San Diego and headed west. Had a short stop at Pearl Harbor, saw the USS Arizona memorial, which at that time was just a small wooden platform with a flag pole. Had a short 6 hour pass to go ashore, but didn't see much since it was at night and about the only things open were the bars, so we headed west again. We flew some patrols and played a few war games with our own ships until we got to Okinawa. I remember we were at Okinawa for

Thanksgiving. That is where things started to get interesting, while we were at

U.S.S. Bataan

Okinawa they got word that a typhoon was headed our way. The captain of the Bataan didn't want to get caught in the harbor when the typhoon hit so we put to sea to try to outrun the typhoon. The first night out was the worse. The ship pitched and rolled and you had to hang on just to stay in your bunk. Anything that wasn't tied down went sliding across the deck. Shoes were going from one side of the room to the other all night and in the morning we had to hunt all over for our own shoes. At one time the ship took a forty-five-degree roll. They said the most the ship could take was 48-degree roll before going over. They had a crew on the flight deck ready to cut our planes loose and push them over the side if we got another roll like that. To relieve some of the weight on top so we wouldn't be so top heavy. We were on cold rations for three days. The ship was rolling and pitching so much the cooks couldn't cook anything and you had to hold on to your food tray while you ate, with one hand or you would lose it

About the only good thing that came about from all that was that while we were trying to out run the typhoon we got close enough to Korea to be in the combat zone and we were all awarded the Korean Service Medal. If that can be considered a good thing. I don't know how close we were to Korea because all I saw was water.

We left Okinawa and went to Japan. Docking in Yokohama. From there we were transferred to a small air base at Atsugi, between Yokohama and Tokyo. We were transported to the base in open trucks and one of the first things I noticed about Japan was that they use every inch of land they could. Houses were built on the side of the hills and mountains and they looked like they sat right on top of each other. The farmland we went past had crops planted right up to the edge of the road. Of course the Japanese all drove on the wrong side of the road and used their horns more that the brakes. All you could hear was horns blasting away.

One day while we were at Atsugi I went on a flight and we went up and flew around the rim of Mt. Fuji. We could look right down into the center of the volcano. I wished I had my camera with me but it was back in the barracks. Another thing I found interesting was their cemeteries. The head stones and markers were so close together I thought that they must buried them standing up. It wasn't until later that I found out they cremate their dead so there were only ashes buried there.

U.S.S. Badoeng Strait

In the spring of 1953 we boarded the aircraft carrier Badoeng Strait for our return to the states. It was a long trip home, we didn't do much except lay around and play cards. We didn't do any flying on our way home and arrived back in Los Alamitos in early March of 1953.

The last year of my service was pretty uneventful. Not much happened and I was lucky enough to spend most of that year on night check duty. Our job was to run routine checks on all our aircraft and have them ready for flying the next morning. We went on duty at 5 P.M. and as soon as all the planes were checked and ready, we were done. Sometimes that would only take an hour or two and we would be back in the barracks by 7 or 8 P.M. If they were doing any night flying we would be there until 10 P.M. or midnight, but never much later. We also got midnight chow which was much better that the regular meals they fixed. I gained about TEN POUNDS that year.

The only injury I received was a dislocated little finger on my right hand, which stills bothers me. I got it from a foul tip while catching in a softball game for our squadron team. They wouldn't give me the Purple Heart for it because they said it wasn't combat related. To me a softball game was combat.

I was discharged on April 18, 1954, even though my enlistment wasn't up until June 20. I was given an early out because my squadron was getting ready to go back over seas. Some of my buddies signed a year's extension so they could go with them. But I just wanted out. My rank at the time of my discharge was Aviation

Electronics Technician Third Class Petty Officer. Our squadron number was changed from VS-871 to VS-37 when we went over seas.

June 20 is a day I always remember. That is the day I joined the Navy just before the Korean War started. And on June 20, 1954 I got married which started another war, but that is another war story for another time.

Chapter Five
The Married Years

When George got out of the Navy in April 1954 he headed for Arizona. He rented a small one-room apartment on Grand Avenue between Camelback Road and Indian School Road. It was close to where Mary lived. George got a job at International Metal Company on South 16th Street in Phoenix. They manufactured air conditioners and swamp coolers for homes and businesses. George worked in the motor room in the shipping department. His job was to receive and inventory the electric motors for the coolers and to make sure when they shipped the coolers that the correct electric motor was shipped with each unit. He worked there for about two months until just before the wedding. Then just about a week before the wedding he got the flu and had to quit. George lost about ten to fifteen pounds, all the extra weight he had gained the last year in the Navy. That is why he looked so thin in all the wedding pictures.

George and Mary were busy getting all the last minute details ready for the wedding. George got a new suit and Mary got her wedding dress. They made arrangements to rent the hall at Immaculate Heart Catholic Church, where they were going to get married, for their reception. Flowers to order, dresses for the bridesmaids, suits for the best men and ushers, and all the other little things that seem to pile up at the last minute and don't forget the marriage license. At last the big day was here, Sunday June 20, 1954 George Davison and Mary Lira were married at the 10:00 A.M. mass at Immaculate Heart Catholic Church on East Washington Street in downtown Phoenix. At least that is what was written on their marriage certificate and what Mary told George. George was never sure what happened; the priest that performed the ceremony didn't speak a word of English and George didn't understand a word of Spanish. When the priest stopped talking and looked at George, Mary poked George in the ribs and George said, "I do." For the next forty-seven years George just assumed they were married but he was never sure.

Oscar brought Grandma, Marie, Wayne, and Karla out to Arizona from Michigan for the wedding. Retta was there too so George had some of his family there for the wedding. Grandma didn't make it to the wedding itself because she couldn't stand the heat. But she was here anyway. After the wedding Oscar and the family went on to California before heading back to Michigan.

After the wedding George and Mary went to Wickenburg for their honeymoon. After a few days in Wickenburg they came back to

Glendale and packed up the car and headed for Michigan where they were going to make their home. They had everything they owned including Mary's hope chest packed in the car when they left Glendale. They took their time on the way to Michigan and did a little sight seeing on the way. They arrived in Michigan the first week in July just after the Forth of July and settled in at Oscar's cottage at Ford Lake until George could find a job and afford a place of their own, which never happened.

When George and Mary got to Michigan, Oscar had another wedding reception for them at the town hall in Fountain. Mary got to meet some of George's friends that he grew up with around Fountain but a lot of them had left the area.

George started looking for a job but he found out things weren't any better then when he had left to join the Navy four years before. None of the factories in Muskegon or Grand Rapids were hiring and there were no jobs available. George was able to pick up some work during haying season on some of the farms around town but just a few days here and there, nothing permanent. Things were not looking good. George went down to Michigan State University to see if he could enroll in college under the GI bill but found out he didn't have the money needed to pay his tuition and the up front cost he would need to start school. So that was out. When the canning factory in Scottville opened up George was able to get a job there but he knew it wouldn't last very long, just through the canning season then it would be over.

One day Mary wanted to make tacos for the family to show the people in Michigan what real Mexican tacos were like. George and Mary went to every store in Mason County but couldn't find any taco shells anywhere. One of the stores said that sometimes they had them when the Mexican labors were there working in the harvest but they didn't have them at that time. So no tacos.

Mary was having a hard time adjusting, she didn't like living in the cabin by the lake. It was to cold and isolated and she didn't have any one to visit. Wayne would ride his bike out to the lake and spend some time with her while George was working but that was about the only company she had. Of course there was no television for her to watch and not much for her to do. Mary started getting homesick for her family and then they discovered she was pregnant. That really compounded her problems. About that time Grandma, Cleo, and Glee each took George aside and had a talk with him. The all told him basically the same thing. "If you want to keep that girl, you had better get her out of here and back to Arizona, she will never survive a winter here in Michigan." So when the canning factory closed the first part of September, George had enough money saved to get them back to Arizona. They packed all their belonging in the car, including Mary's hope chest and headed back to Arizona. They had to ship a couple of boxes because they didn't have room for everything in the car. They had more stuff to take back than they had brought with them because they had received some gifts at the reception Oscar had for them and George had his guns and some clothes and other thing he had left behind when he joined the Navy.

They didn't know what would lie ahead for them when they got back to Arizona. Mary knew she would be able to go back to work at Good Samaritan Hospital and George was hopeful that he would be able to find some kind of work. It couldn't be any worse that it was in Michigan and there must be a job waiting for him somewhere. He would just have to start looking and hope something would turn up. Mary was happy to be heading home to her family and they made the long drive back to Arizona with out any trouble.

Things started looking up for them when they got back to Arizona. Mary got her job back at Good Samaritan Hospital, they were glad to see her back. George was able to find a job in

less that a week as an assistant manager at the Strand Theatre in downtown Phoenix. They rented a small apartment on the corner of Brill

Street and Tenth Street right across the street from the hospital so Mary was able to walk to work, she didn't drive at that time. Mary liked the idea of George working in the theatre now she could go to the movies anytime she wanted to, all she needed was fifteen cents for popcorn and a dime for a coke, she got in free. George could also get her free passes to the other theatres around town if she didn't like what was showing at the Strand.

    The Strand Theatre was owned by the Paramount Theatre Corporation, which had four other theatres in Phoenix and two in Tucson. Beside the Strand which was one on West Washington right across the street from the old courthouse. There was the Realto Theatre also located downtown, The Palms Theatre on North Central and Palm Lane, The Indian Drive-in Theatre located at the corner of Indian School Road and Twenty-seventh Avenue and the Paramount Theatre located on the corner of Adams and Second Avenue. All the theatres are gone now except the Paramount, which is now the restored Orpheum Theatre.

    The hours were long and the pay wasn't that great, George started at $30.00 a week but got a raise to $35.00 within a month. His day would start sometime between 11 AM and noon to get things set up and ready to open for the first showing which usually started between 12 and 12:30 and he would be there to lock up after the last show which sometimes could be as late as midnight. Sometimes he would get two or three hours off in the middle of the afternoon and he and the manager would take turns staying late to lock up during the week but they both stayed until closing on weekends. Six days a week and no holidays or weekends off, they were our busiest days.

Some of George's duties included doing the payroll, checking out the cashiers and the candy counter girls at the end of their shift. Making up the bank deposit and taking it to the bank. We had a security guard that came by and escorted us to the bank every night to put our deposit in the night drop. Then the next day we would go to the bank and make our deposit. There were daily reports to make on our ticket sales and sales from the candy counter that had to go to the main office after the close of business each day. George would have to take inventory and order the candy and supplies needed for the candy counter from the company warehouse once a week. During intermission George would help the girl at the candy counter keep up with the rush of customers. George had to wear a tie and sometimes when he was working behind the candy counter he would end up stuffing his tie in a box of popcorn or dipping the end of it in a cup of soda. He soon got tired of that and went out and brought himself some bow ties and that is what he wore for years after that even after he left the theatres. George would also relieve the cashier and the candy counter girl when they took a break. George also had to make the schedule for the movie, what time to start each feature, how long an intermission between shows, which short features to run and at what times. He also had to draw up the display that they were to put up on the marquee each time they changed movies. Thank goodness he didn't have to climb up on a ladder and change the marquee himself, one of the custodians did that.

George was a fast learner and it didn't take him long to learn his job and what was expected of him, which was a good thing. He had only been there a little over a month when they had a shake up over at the Paramount Theatre. The manager and the assistant manager were both fired, we heard there was some hankie panky going on between them and some of the female employees. The district office transferred the manager of the Strand over there as interim manager until they could hire a new manager and left George in charge of the Strand. George managed the Strand for the next four weeks with out a day off. If something came up he wasn't familiar with or he had a question about something, he could always call his manager to get help but he was pretty much on his own.

George got through the four weeks with only a couple of incidents. The first one happened when one of the cashiers called in sick one day. Later someone told George they had seen her at the fair with her husband and son when she was suppose to be working or home sick. That got George upset and made him mad. He was trying to run the theatre with a small staff to start with and the manager was gone so that really left them short handed. The next day when the cashier showed up for her shift George told her she was fired. She was upset and later that night her husband came to the theatre and was going to beat up on George if he didn't give her back her job. George held his ground and refused to hire her back and her husband finally left with out any blows being thrown. George had some application on file for cashiers and he called a couple of them to come in for an interview and the next day he hired a new cashier to replace her.

The second incident happened when George got up one morning with a sore throat and a fever. His tonsils were acting up again like they did when he was in the Navy. Mary didn't want him to go to work but he knew there was no one else to open the theatre and take over so he took a couple of aspirin and went to work anyway. George got the theatre open and ready for business, went to the bank and did the banking then he told the girls how bad he was feeling. The usherette that was on duty said that she would relieve the cashier and candy girl for their breaks so George wouldn't have to and the girls all agreed they would cover for him. George told them he would be in the office if they needed him for anything. Then he spent most of the day sleeping in the office. The girls kept things under control that day and George was able to get some rest. They were a great bunch to be working with. The next day George felt better and it was back to business as usual.

One night we were showing "Gone With The Wind." It was a long movie, about four hours long with an intermission about half way through. George was standing by the door when a couple came up to him and asked what time the second part started. They had seen the first part at another theatre but they left at the intermission thinking it was the end of the movie. They found out later they had only seen half of the movie and now wanted to see the end. One weekend we were showing a cartoon marathon, four hours of nothing but cartoons. We were use to people dropping their kids off at the theatre for us to baby sit until the movie was over but that weekend was something else. The theatre was packed with mostly kids that weekend. The adults that were there seemed to enjoy it as much as the kids. George remembers one older man that appeared to be there by himself. You could hear him laugh all over the theatre and he would sit there and stomp his feet and slap his hands on his knees. He really enjoyed it.

The end of November or first part of December they hired a new manager for the Paramount Theatre and the manager of the Strand came back to take over. Things were back to normal again for a couple of weeks. They still didn't have an assistant manager for the Paramount. So they offered George the job as assistant manager at the Paramount Theatre, which also meant a raise in pay, so George took the job. He was now making $40.00 a week. His duties were basically the same as they had been at the Strand. There were more employees to supervise and more responsibility, since it was a much larger theatre. After the first of the year George got another raise to $45.00 a week, that was top pay at the time and that is what he earned for the next eight months.

They had a good crew at the Paramount and George got along well with all of them. One day George was coming down the stairs from the office, about half way down he came to the landing in the stairway. He had a good view of the lobby below and saw two of the usherettes standing by the candy counter talking to the candy counter girl. They were supposed to be in the main theatre keeping an eye on the people. They were talking and laughing and having a good time. George just stopped on the landing and stood there with his arms crossed looking at them. After about a minute they stopped talking and it was so quiet you could have heard a pin drop in the lobby. They must have sensed that George was watching them. Three heads turned at once and looked up to where George was standing. Then with out another word the usherettes hurried back to their post and the candy counter girl acted busy cleaning and straightening up behind the candy counter. George proceeded down the stairs and went on about his business. He never said a word to any of them, he didn't have to, and they knew what they had done wrong. It was not a very busy day and there was no harm done.

    Sometimes at night when we had a large crowd we would open up the side doors in the lobby during intermission to let the people out for a cigarette. George would stand outside to keep an eye on everyone and make sure no one tried to sneak in without a ticket. One night George was standing out there and he saw a man coming up the sidewalk from down the street. The man was staggering a little and looked like he had been drinking, he was a big man over six feet tall. Just as George suspected the man tried to sneak in one of the open doors. George headed him off and stopped him and told him he couldn't come in. The man tried to convince George he had just stepped out for a cigarette. George asked him for his ticket stub and he said he must have dropped it somewhere. He tried to push his way passed George but George wouldn't let him in. Just when it looked like things could get ugly the manager came up behind George and wanted to know what the problem was. George told him what had happened and the manager told the man that he had better leave or we would call the police. The man left without another word.

Maria was born in March 1955 and Mary gave up her job at the hospital to be a stay-at-home mother. At least for the time being. George continued his work at the theatre and early in the summer they were able to purchase a small one-bedroom house at 3607 West Melvin Street, just one block north of Van Buren Street. At that time it was just outside of the Phoenix City limits. That would be their home for the next four years.

That summer Mary convinced George that he should go to college, under the GI Bill. George quit his job at the theatre and enrolled at Phoenix College for the fall semester in 1955. Mary went back to work at Good Samaritan Hospital, on the evening shift 3:00 PM to 11:30 PM. George was able to schedule all his classes early in the day. That way he could be home in time to take Mary to work, she didn't drive. After taking Mary to work George would come home and do his homework and take care of Maria and then pick Mary up when she got off work. It could make for a long day. Some of his classes would start as early as 7:00 AM. Thank goodness it wasn't everyday that they started that early.

One morning George overslept. His first class that day was algebra and he knew they were having a mid-term exam that morning. He dressed in a hurry and rushed off to school with out even stopping to wash his face or brush his teeth. He was about fifteen minutes late and when he got his test he discovered it consisted of ten problems each worth ten points. He went to work and finished as many as he could before he ran out of time. He only got eight of the ten problems done but ended up getting an eighty on the test. If he hadn't overslept he might have gotten a one hundred on that test.

The first year George had a physiology professor that just about drove him crazy. She used the phase "You see." Or "You know" to end every statement she made during her lectures. George tried to count how many times she used the phase one-day but lost track. George was happy when that class was over. It was driving him up the wall "you know."

George was having the most trouble with his English class. He couldn't tell a proper noun from an improper noun, a preposition from a proposition. Adverbs, adjectives, they were all the same to him. And of course his spelling was terrible, he had always been a poor speller. Mary had to correct the spelling on any reports he had to write before he could turn them in. He was struggling with that class until one day Mr. Franks, the professor, brought in a recording of OTHELLO by William Shakespeare for the class to listen to and discuss. They played a little of it the first day and then discussed what they had heard. They were going to continue on with it the rest of the week. After class George went to the library and checked out a copy of the play and took it home and read part of it that night. The next day in class, after they listened to some more of it and were getting ready to start their discussion. George asked Mr. Franks if they hadn't left out one of the scenes on the recording. Mr. Franks asked George how he knew that. George told him what he had done. Mr. Franks looked at George in disbelief and he shouted at George "You did what?" George repeated what he had said before. Mr. Franks then asked "Why?" George said that he thought he would be able to understand it better if he could read along as they were playing the recording. The way Mr. Franks was yelling and carrying on, George thought he was in big trouble. Mr. Franks then turned to the rest of the class and asked if any of them had bothered to check out a copy from the library, he was sure they had more than one copy. No one had, but the next day about half the class showed up with a copy of the play. George realized then that Mr. Franks wasn't mad at him, it was just his way of showing his approval for what George had done. George became the teachers pet after that and he is sure that what he did that day is what got him through the class with a passing grade. Mr. Franks talked to George after the final exams that semester and told him he would like to be able to give George a higher grade but George did so badly on the test that a C was the best he could do.

George started out to get his degree in Business Administration with a major in Business Management. By the end of the first year he decided to switch his major to Accounting. He figured he was better suited for a career in that field than in management. Also he enjoyed working with figures, whether they were on paper or in a skirt.

George wasn't the smartest kid in school but by working hard and putting in a little extra effort he was able to get good grades. He graduated from Phoenix College with an Associate in Arts Degree with high distinction in May of 1957. He was admitted to Iota Sigma Alpha, an honor society for having such good grades. Most of his grades were straight A's, with a couple of B's, except for his C in English.

The spring of 1957 George had his tonsils removed; they had been bothering him off and on since he was in the Navy. He was able to have it done on a Friday morning and was back in class on Monday so he only missed one day of classes.

The summers of 1956 and 1957 George got a summer job at Wright Manufacturing Company. They made evaporative coolers and air conditioners. George worked in the sheet metal department operating power shears, punch presses, and other equipment forming metal parts for the coolers. He worked the night shift from 6:00 PM to 6:00 AM five nights a week and on Saturday night; they worked from 5:00 PM to midnight. They didn't want to pay double time for working on Sundays. The pay was good but the hours were long and it was hard sleeping during the day.

The fall of 1957 George transferred to Arizona State College at Tempe to complete his education and get his degree in Accounting. During his senior year the name of the school was changed to Arizona State University so George was in the first graduating class at Arizona State University. The summer of 1958 George took a couple of summer school classes to pick up a couple of classes he needed for graduation but hadn't been able to work into his schedule during the regular school year. George also got a part time job as a bookkeeper for an insurance agency, so he was pretty busy.

Cindy was born in November 1958. George had a midterm exam in one of his classes that morning. He took Mary to the hospital then ran off to school to take his test. As soon as the test was over he hurried back to the hospital and skipped the rest of his classes for that day. Cindy waited until George got back to the hospital before she was born.

Now that they had two small children Mary gave up her job at the hospital. Money was tight; the GI bill only went so far, so George had to get a part time job to make ends meet. George got a job in the snack bar at the Acres Drive-in Theatre. It was just a couple of blocks from where they lived. The hours were perfect for some one going to school, 6:30 PM to about 11:00 PM or midnight. Everyone that worked there had another job and worked there as a second job to supplement their income. They were all men. Because of George's previous experience in the theatre he was soon promoted to assistant snack bar manager. POPCORN, SODA, HOTDOGS "Do you want that with or without chili?" PIZZA, TAMALES. George sold them all. Of course he also had to take inventory and balance out the cash register at the end of the shift.

In May 1959, George graduated from Arizona State University with a Bachelor of Science Degree with Distinction in Business Administration with a major in Accounting. Again he had been able to keep his grades up and except for a C in biology the rest of his grades were all A's and B's. His father came out for his graduation. The university had a banquet for all the married students and the wives all received a PHT degree: PUSHING HUBBY THROUGH. Mary sure deserved it, George said that he never would have made it without her help and encouragement.

Now that he was through school and had his degree Mary expected him to get a job and go to work. What a bummer. The school set up interviews for the graduates with different companies. All the large accounting firms came on campus to interview the accounting students. George had some interviews with them but they didn't go very well. One of the questions that George would always ask them was how much travel is involved and how much time would he spend on the road. In just about every case they said you could expect to spend anywhere from 25% to 50% of the time on the road. Some of the larger CPA firms even said that you would have to go back east for about six months training at their home offices. Since George had a wife and two small children, he didn't want to spend that much time away from his family. He was hoping to find something where he would be able to spend more time at home and not have to travel.

George heard about a couple of jobs that wouldn't require so much travel. One was with the City of Glendale and the other was with the Mohawk Irrigation District. George put in an application with both of them. The Mohawk Irrigation District was located in Wellton in the southwest part of the state about twenty miles east of Yuma. That was about one hundred and seventy-five miles from Phoenix. George drove down there for an interview. There was not much there at that time, just a small town on the side of the road. There was very little housing available in town and the irrigation district had its own housing available for their employees, which you could rent for a nominal fee. They sat right out in the desert with no trees or anything around them. It was a growing community and the potential for the area looked good. They liked George and offered him a job starting at $400.00 a month. George wasn't sure if Mary would like it there or not; it would be quite a ways away from her family. Also they would have to sell their house in Phoenix. So George asked for $450.00 a month to start. They couldn't come to an agreement so George drove back to Phoenix. When he got home Mary said the City of Glendale had called and wanted him to come in for an interview the next day. The next morning George went for an interview with the City Of Glendale. They offered George a job starting at $400.00 a month and George took it. When George got back home after accepting the job with Glendale, Mary said that the Mohawk Irrigation District had called. George called them back and they said that they had gotten approval from their board of directors to pay the $450.00 that George was asking. George had to tell them he was sorry but he had just taken a job with the City of Glendale. That job only lasted for twenty-eight years, maybe the other one would have lasted longer.

The last semester of college George had taken a graduate course in Governmental Accounting, which was not a required course. Of course both the city and the irrigation district used governmental accounting which is much different that accounting for a business. That may be why George was so lucky to have been offered both of those jobs.

July 1, 1959 George went to work as an accountant for the City of Glendale. George was the first accountant that the city had ever had. The city manager had a background in accounting and did some of the accounting work prior to George being hired. The city treasurer, who handled the city's finances and the day-to-day bookkeeping work, was a retired college history professor. He knew nothing about accounting and had been appointed treasurer because he had some friends on the city council. The city manager was fired about nine months after George was hired and the chief of police was appointed the new city manager. He knew nothing about accounting either so that left George as the only one with any accounting experience or knowledge. George was able to bluff his way through and make people believe he knew what he was doing.

Over the next twenty-eight years George's duties were many and varied as the city grew and his responsibility's changed. Some of his duties over the years included preparing the city budget, making revenue and expenditures projections, and preparing reports for the state and federal government. At one time every bill that the city paid had to be approved by George before they could write a check. George would have to make sure all the proper paper work and authorization's were in

THE City of Glendale Accounting Department!

place and assign an account number so the proper department was charged for each expenditure. As the city grew jobs would have to be reassigned and part of George's responsibility would be to make sure accounting checks and balances were all in place. Forms would have to be changed and redesigned, there was always something new, and it wasn't the same old routine day after day.

George became the go-to-guy whenever anyone had a problem with their record keeping or balancing their books. Police department, fire department, city court, payroll clerk, utility billing, cashiers; George helped them all at one time or another with their accounting problems. He had the ability to analyze the problem and help them find a solution. His last boss said that George had one of the most analytic minds he had ever know. Whatever that meant, George took it as a complement. One time the city was going to change the forms they were using for their utility billing. They were going to include a return envelope with the bill for customers to use to mail in their payments. They had different companies come in to help them redesign the forms. One of the companies was making their presentation when George noticed that the return envelope they had looked kind of small. He compared it to a check and sure enough you couldn't put a personal check in it without folding the check. George said that would make a lot more work for the people opening and processing the mail payments if they had to unfold every check. It would take more time and the checks would be harder to handle. The company went back and redesigned the form and the return envelope. It was the little things like that George had the ability to spot and to get corrected before they became a big problem.

George kept his part time job at the snack bar at the theatre for about 3 years. He enjoyed working there and had made many friends. He did cut back his hours to only two or three nights a week. Mary and the girls liked it to because they could go to the movies free while George was working there.

One of the requirements for working at the City of Glendale at that time was that you had to live in the City of Glendale. They gave George six months after he started working to move. George started looking for a house to buy in Glendale. One of the builders was building some new homes in Glendale at that time and George was able to qualify for one of those homes for $11,150.00. They were able to watch it go up from the time the foundation was poured until the house was completed in mid-November. Thanksgiving weekend, 1959, George, Mary and the girls moved into a brand new three-bedroom home at 1726 East Orange Lane. In about 1963 the city changed the street name and address to conform to the county-wide street and address naming system and the address was changed to 4901 West Krall Street. Same house, same location just a different address. That would be their home for the next forty-five plus years and still counting.

They made some improvements over the years. One of the first things they had to do was get wall to wall drapes installed in the living room and dining area. Then they fenced in the back yard so they wouldn't have to keep the dog tied up all the time. They added a large fifteen by thirty-foot patio on the back. Carpet was installed one or two rooms at a time until the whole house was carpeted. Later they had the front yard fenced. In the early 1970's George's mother and stepfather started coming out from Michigan for the winters so George added another fifteen by twenty room on the back so they would have a place to stay. In 1988 they started having problems with the furnace so George had the furnace taken out and replaced it with a heat pump, heating and refrigeration unit. Now after thirty years they had air conditioning, prior to that they had to try and keep the house cool with a swamp cooler, which worked fine most of the time except when the humidity was high.

George and Mary kept the house on Melvin Street and used it as a rental until 1965. By then the neighborhood was getting run down, the house needed some repairs and it was getting hard to find and keep good renters so they sold the house.

George and the family would make frequent trips back to Michigan to see his family about every two or three years. Four times they went by train. They liked traveling by train and the girls enjoyed it when they were small. When the girls got older they drove to Michigan four times. In 1968 they went to George's high school class reunion. George introduced Mary as his wife, Maria Guadalupe Jimenez Lira. Mary could have killed George for that. George said he though it had a nice poetic ring to it. Mary didn't think so. The last time they went as a family was in 1972, Maria had her driver's license that year and helped George with the driving. After that George would usually make the trip by himself and would fly rather than drive.

Family Portrait, circa 1976

In 1974 Grandma was in and out of a coma and wasn't expected to live much longer. George flew back to Michigan and Wayne took him up to Ludington to see her. They went to the nursing home and spent some time with her but she didn't respond to anything they said. They left and said they would be back later. Cleo or Glee was staying with her and they said that after George left Grandma woke up and said, "George was here wasn't he?" When George got back to the nursing home

130

later that afternoon Grandma was awake and wanted to know if Mary and the girls had come with him and how they were doing. They had a nice visit. Grandma lived another year after that and when she died in 1975 George went back for the funeral and was one of her pall-bearers.

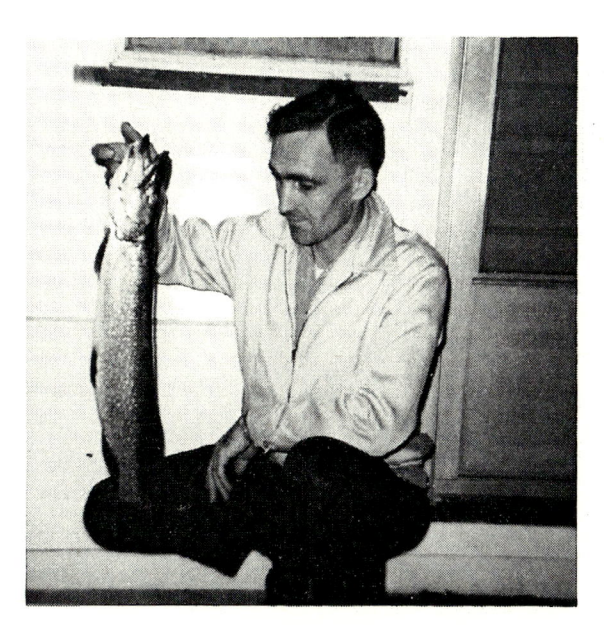

In 1978 Cyndy went to Michigan with him. They went to the Davison reunion and Wayne took them to a ballgame in Detroit. The fall of 1979, George went back to Michigan to go deer hunting with Wayne and the rest of the family; it had been thirty years since he had hunted in Michigan. He didn't get a deer. The summer of 1984, George, Wayne and their brother-in-law Jack took Oscar to Canada to go fishing. Oscar had been diagnosed with cancer and wanted to make one more fishing trip to Canada to catch some walleye. They got him up to Canada all right but they never got him out on the lake. He was too tired. The fishing wasn't that good either they caught a couple of pike but no walleye. George didn't catch a thing. In 1986, Mary and George both went back to Michigan for Christmas. It was the first time they had been back there in the wintertime and they both just about froze to death.

George and Mary became chartered members of St. Louis the King Catholic Church when it was established in 1962. Over the years they were both involved in different works at the church. Mary was very active in the Women's Club. George taught religious education classes when the girls were in grade school. Later, when they were in high school, Mary and George both worked with the youth group. George also served as an usher and as an Eucharistic minister. They both helped with the bingo games when the church had them.

As the girls were growing up, Mary and George encouraged them to get involved in as many different activities as possible. They took swimming lessons, were in the girl scouts, and went to scout camp. Maria enjoyed her time at camp, Cyndy did not, and she got sick when she was at camp. George and Mary were scout leaders for a few years when they first started. Maria stayed in scouting until she was in high school. Cyndy dropped out after the first few years. They took piano and dancing lessons. Maria continued on with her piano all the way through college and became a music teacher at an elementary school and plays the piano for church services. Cyndy took the other road, she loved to dance. She danced on the pomp line in grade school and high school. She studied dancing in college and taught dancing part time. Cyndy appeared in quite a few plays around the valley for different theatrical groups as a dancer, singer and actress. She even did some choreography for some of the plays she was in. Sports were the same way, one went one way and the other went the other way. They both played softball and George was their coach when they both started. George started out coaching Maria's team and when she got older and moved up into a higher league he coached Cyndy's team. Maria played softball until she was in high school; she also played a little tennis in high school. Cyndy enjoyed running track more than playing softball. She ran track in grade school, high school and was on the ASU track team when she was in college. Maria got her degree in Music Education and Cyndy got her degree in Physical Education. Maria went on to teach in the grade school and Cyndy never taught at all.

    In 1963 or 1964 Mary wanted to get her drivers license so George set out to teach her to drive. One day they were returning from one of her lessons and she came in the driveway too fast and ran right in to the storeroom at the end of the carport. She said, "I will never be able to drive." George said "Yes, you will." He made her back the car out of the driveway and drive around the block and back into the carport before he would let her go in the house. She got her license shortly after that, even though she never learned to parallel park.

Mary wanted to keep her nursing license active and to do that she would have to work so many hours every few years. So when the girls got older she went back to work. She worked part time for a couple of years at Good Samaritan Hospital, Friday and Saturday nights from 11:00 PM to 7:00 AM, that way George would be home with the girls. They would all be sleeping anyway. In 1964 they built and opened a new hospital in Glendale and she got a job there working the same hours. She didn't like it there too much, she said they expected too much. Some times she would be the only RN in the whole hospital on the night shift. So she left there and went to work at John C. Lincoln Hospital in Sunnyslope. She liked it there a lot better. She worked there two or three years, the same night shift she had been working before, two or three nights a week.

Things were going well until the day she turned 40, June 23, 1966. That night, on the way to work, she was feeling depressed, she didn't want to be forty; that was old. She was crying about it as she drove and then she was stopped at a stoplight. A car with a group of young teenage boys pulled up beside her. They started whistling at her and one of them shouted, "Hi cutie." She started crying all the harder. Eventually she got over it and accepted the fact that forty wasn't old.

Mary had been active in the school PTA and as a homeroom mother at Unit 4 school. So in the summer of 1967, when the school nurse left, Mr. Sine, the principal told Mary he wanted her to apply for the job. Mary said she didn't know anything about school nursing but

Mr. Sine said he had seen the way she reacted around the kids and she would do just fine. So Mary put in her application. Then she had to go for an interview with Glenn Burton, the district superintendent. Mary's father had worked for Mr. Burton's father and lived on their farm for awhile when Mary was small. They spent most of the time talking about the people they knew and what things were like when they were young. Finally Mary asked him about the job and he said "The job is yours and you will do just fine." That was it.

September 1967, Mary started as school nurse at Unit 4 school, later to be renamed to Melvin E. Sine School. That is where she would spend the next 19 years. The hours were perfect the girls would go to school with her in the morning, and wait after school and come home with her at the end of the day. When they were out of school she would be off also. There were a few days at the beginning and end of each school year when she would have to work and the girls would not have school but not very many. Mary enjoyed working with the kids, especially the younger ones, some of the older ones would give her problems once in a while but the first, second, and third, graders were precious. She took care of all their scrapes, cuts and bruises. She made sure they took their medication if they needed it and listened to their problems. She was also in charge of the free lunch program for those who couldn't afford to pay for their lunches. The parents would have to come in and sign up for the program and she would have to make sure all the paper work was done and turned in. If someone forgot his or her lunch money or misplaced their lunch ticket, "Go and see Mrs. Davison." She didn't let any of them go hungry even if it had to come out of her own pocket.

Mary's biggest crisis as a school nurse came one day at recess time when someone came running into her office and said that some one had fallen off the monkey bars and broke her arm. Mary went running out to the playground to take care of it. When she got there she went into shock. It wasn't just another kid that had gotten hurt; it was her daughter, Cyndy. At that moment she was no longer dependable Nurse Mary, now she was just another panicky mother whose little girl had been hurt. The principal and one of the teachers had to take over. They carried Cyndy to the office, called for an ambulance to take Cyndy to the hospital and called George at work. George met them at the hospital. Mr. Sine said that was the only crisis they had at school that Mary wasn't able to handle.

At the end of the school year in June 1986 Mary retired after 19 years as school nurse. She hadn't been feeling to well the last year and she was just a few weeks shy of her sixtieth birthday at which time she would be able to start drawing her retirement. So she took an early retirement.

Meanwhile back at city hall things weren't going so good for George. George had some differences of opinion with the director of computer services who wanted to do things his way and would make changes to some of the accounting programs with out checking with the accounting department first. They clashed on a number of issues. Then the city went out and leased a computer program that was to do all the general ledger accounting and the payroll for the city. It would take the place of all the hand posted ledgers. The theory was good and would save a lot of work supposedly. However the program was so full of bugs and they had so much trouble with it that it never did work properly. George was spending most of his time going through computer printouts trying to figure out why nothing would balance. Once he found a problem and reported it to his boss and the computer department, they would have to send it back to the company they leased the program from and wait for them to make the correction in the program. The city's computer programmers couldn't touch it or do anything about it. The payroll was also a mess and George would have to work with the people in the payroll department helping them find and correct the errors in the payroll. George was getting flustered and fought it for three years, then he took an early retirement. After George left the head of the payroll department lasted about three months, then she left too. She said that after George retired she couldn't get any help and the payroll was in such disarray she couldn't take it anymore. About three or four years after George left, he heard that they did away with that program and got a new one. They never could get it to work properly.

  July 1, 1987 George retired at the age of fifty-seven years with twenty-eight years with the City of Glendale. He wanted to get in his thirty years but just couldn't take the hassle any more. He had his eighty-five points that he needed to draw his full retirement benefits from the state retirement system. Years of service—twenty-eight plus age fifty seven equaled eighty-five so goodbye headaches. Mary had

Happy in Retirement

retired a year earlier so now they could spend more time together and enjoy their retirement home in the mountains at Yarnell.

George and Mary were never sorry that they took an early retirement. The first two years they were busier than ever. Mary's father was in failing health, he had a live in housekeeper, but couldn't drive anymore. He needed some one to take him to the doctors, the bank, and to the store. Mary took him by herself the first year and after George retired they both took him when he had to get out and around. They even started doing his shopping for him when he got to where he couldn't make it to the store anymore. He passed away in June of 1988. After he passed away George went back to Michigan to spend some time with his father and family. George spent over a month in Michigan going to the family reunion and his high school class reunion. Shortly after George got back from Michigan he learned that his father's cancer had returned so he and Mary both went back to Michigan in September to be there for his father's birthday and help take care of him. They came back to Arizona in October and in November when his father got worse George went back to Michigan. His father passed away the first part of December 1988 and Mary and Cyndy flew back for the funeral. Then they all returned to Arizona. So Mary and George both lost their fathers that year.

When Mary retired she started taking an aerobics class at the senior center, when George retired she talked him in to joining her. They both got involved in other activities at the center. They served on an advisory committee helping to plan activities at the center. They would help put on the activities, took a few trips with groups from the center and found themselves busy with whatever the staff needed help with. George would even lead the aerobics class when the regular instructor couldn't be there.

In 1985 George and Mary purchased a house in Yarnell for a summer home and a place to spend part of their retirement. Mary had always wanted a house on top of a hill, now she had one on top of a mountain. Well it may not have been on top of the mountain; Yarnell sat in a small valley near the top of the mountain. So it was close to the top. It was a small one-bedroom house with a large 12 by 24 room addition on the back so there was plenty of room for the family when the kids and grandkids came. Now George and Mary started spending more time there, traveling back and

forth between Glendale and Yarnell. It was just a seventy-five-mile trip one way. While in Yarnell George and Mary got involved with the Shrine of St. Joseph of the Mountain. George served on the board of directors as treasurer for six years from 1990 to 1996. They both helped run the gift shop at the Shrine when they were in Yarnell and did other work around the Shrine as needed.

    In 1989 Mary was diagnosed with Lupus, she took it hard at first but they joined a support group and learned to cope with it. With the proper medication and getting plenty of rest she was able to keep it under control. It did slow her down a bit but it didn't stop her, she still kept going. Grandkids ball games, recitals, plays, graduations, whatever, she was still there for them. If they weren't traveling back and forth to Yarnell they were traveling back and forth to Chandler and still keeping busy at the senior center.

The summer of 1997, George and Mary had been retired for ten years and enjoying every minute of it. They were merrily rolling along on the retirement wagon. Then the end of June the wheels fell off the wagon. Mary started having chest pains, a trip to the family doctor and an EKG confirmed what they both suspected Mary had had a minor heart attack. She was referred to a heart specialist. Two days later more chest pains, a trip to the emergency room, she was stabilized and sent home. Two days later at the heart specialist office, there were more tests; they were inconclusive, something was wrong but the doctor couldn't tell for sure what was causing it. He would make arrangements to have Mary admitted to the hospital so he could run some more tests. Mary was admitted to the hospital the evening of July 3, 1997.

July 4, 1997 they ran some more tests in the morning, the problem was discovered, three blocked arteries. Open-heart surgery was needed, a triple by-pass was scheduled for that afternoon. After the surgery Mary was in and out of ICU. She had trouble eating and keeping it down, what went down came up. Gallstones were discovered so back to surgery to remove the gallstones. That didn't help much because she still had trouble eating and keeping it down. The end of July she was transferred to a rehabilitation care center, she was there two weeks and things didn't improve; she was getting worse so back to the hospital. She still had trouble eating. One evening George returned to her room after supper and found her lying in a pool of blood. She was having internal bleeding. Lesions were discovered in her intestinal tract, they had to cauterize them to stop the bleeding. Meanwhile she had lost a lot of blood so blood transfusions were started. The next two and a half months were touch and go, they thought there were going to lose her more than once. Finally at the end of October, just about four months after her surgery she was stabilized enough to go home.

October 29, 1997 Mary came home from the hospital; she was still a long way from being back on her feet. She still couldn't eat and came home with a feeding tube in her stomach. George had to pump Ensure into her stomach with a syringe to keep her from starving to death. Arrangements were made for a visiting nurse to come by at least once a week and she was on call if they needed her more often. A nurse's aid came every other day to give her a bath and change her and the bed. A physical therapist and an occupational therapist both came once a week to help her get back on her feet. That arrangement continued for four months until the end of February 1998. She was getting a little stronger by then and was able to get around the house with the aid of a walker. She was also able to start eating soft foods again and in April the feeding tube was removed.

Mary never completely regained her strength, she could get around the house most of the time with the walker. At times she would have to use the wheelchair. About the only times she got out of the house was to go to the doctor. A trip to the doctor required the use of the wheelchair. A couple of times she felt well enough to make it to church and she wanted to go back up to Yarnell. George loaded her in the truck and took her to Yarnell. Once they got there George helped her into the house and got her settled on the couch, where she spent the next two days until they got ready to return to Glendale. Things were never the same after the surgery. Mary spent most of the time on the couch watching television.

The hardest thing for George to cope with was when Mary's mind started to wander and she started having hallucinations. She wouldn't know where she was or what was going on. The periods would come and go. Some days she would be fine, other days she didn't know what she was doing half of the time. They were never able to figure out what caused it, it may have been her medication or it may have been caused by her lupus, they were never sure which. One day George left Mary alone while he went to church, she had been doing good and would be all right for an hour. When George got home from church Mary was in tears she said, "Where were you? Where did you go? I looked all over for you and couldn't find you." George said, "I went to church." Mary said, "That's right, you told me but I forgot." George never left Mary alone after that, if he couldn't find some one to stay with her he didn't go anywhere. One of her sisters would come and stay with Mary one afternoon every week so George could go get groceries and run any errands he had to do. Sometime she would come Saturday evenings so George could go to church. Maria and Cyndy would also come over on weekends and stay with her so George could get out of the house for awhile.

June 2000, Mary fell and broke her pelvis, a couple of days in the hospital and a week in a nursing home, them she was home again. But things were never the same after that. She was getting weaker and not as active as she had been. More doctors, different medications nothing seemed to be helping.

August 9, 2001 Mary had a very bad day; she didn't want to eat and slept most of the day. That night when they went to bed Mary asked George, "Are we going to make it?" George lied and said, "Yes we will make it." The next morning, August 10, when George woke up he didn't like the way she was breathing. George called the paramedics, it didn't take them long to get there but it was too late, Mary was gone by the time they arrived.

After Mary passed away George knew that he had to keep busy and active. He went back to the senior center and started taking the aerobics class he and Mary were taking before she got sick. George got caught up with all the trimming and yard work he had to let go while he was taking care of Mary. Then he went to work cleaning out the attic and the storeroom. He was surprised at how much stuff you could accumulate after forty-two years in the same house. He had a yard sale to get rid of some of it, gave some of it away, and hauled a couple of loads to the dump. Mary had boxes and boxes of papers she was saving until she had time to sort them out so George started sorting and ended up throwing away most of it.

Once George got caught up with all the work around the house, he started spending more time at the senior center. He started eating his noon meal there three or four times a week. He went to aerobics class three days a week and enjoyed sitting around visiting with the girls. About every three months he would take a trip to one of the casinos with a group from the center. He was able to make a few new friends. The center offered a course in computer basics and word processing so George signed up for it. Maria and Bob had an old computer they were not using any more so they brought it over and set it up for George. That is how George got started with his writings.

George made a few trips to his house in Yarnell but it just wasn't the same without Mary. Most of the people they knew up there had left and there just wasn't anyone around there that he knew anymore. He kept the house in Yarnell because Maria and her family enjoyed going up there but he doesn't get up there very much any more. George started playing a little golf again during the wintertime but in the summertime it was too hot. He never got to be very good at it but it was something to do and got him out of the house for awhile.

Chapter Six
Deer Hunting, Arizona Style

The fall of 1959 George started getting the urge to go deer hunting. He hadn't been hunting since 1949. Being in the Navy and going to college didn't give him any opportunities to go hunting. Now that he had that all behind him it was time to get started again. Deer season in Arizona always opened the last Friday in October. So when he heard others talking about deer hunting he decided he would give it a try. He got his license and a box of shells, he had brought his rifle—a 30-40 Winchester--with him from Michigan. He got up early Saturday morning the first weekend of season. He started up the Black Canyon Highway toward Flagstaff. He didn't have any idea where he was going or what to expect. It just felt good to be going hunting again. He didn't know anyone well enough to ask someone to go with him or ask them where to hunt. One of his neighbors just told him to head north so he did. About eighty-five miles north of Phoenix just before he got to the hill dropping down into Camp Verde he saw what looked like it might be a good place to start. He parked his car in a rest area along the highway and started out about an hour after daybreak. He spent most of the morning hunting on the east side of the highway then after lunch he dropped down into a dry creek bed that ran under the highway and crossed over to the west side of the highway through a huge tunnel. He worked his way along the creek bed for about a quarter of a mile and came to a small grove of trees. It had rained the night before so you could walk along without making too much noise. There was some thick brush on the side of the ridge along the creek bed and George was about half way through the grove of trees when he thought he heard something in the brush. He couldn't see anything so he kept working his way along the creek bed real slow looking up the side of the ridge every change he got. When he got to the end of the brush and was able to see around the corner of it. He looked back and saw a nice buck standing about half way up the ridge about fifty yards away. The buck was just standing there looking down towards the creek bottom. George dropped down on one knee, took careful aim and dropped the buck right where it was standing. After he cleaned it out George was trying to shake some of the blood off his hands and his college ring came off and went bouncing down the ridge. George thought sure he had lost it but he was able to recover it. It took George most of the afternoon to drag the buck back to the highway. He would leave his gun and backpack and drag the buck about fifty or seventy-five feet then go back and get his gun and backpack. He would carry them up ahead about the same distance and then go back for the deer, drag it up to that spot then rest and drag again. George kept doing that until he got back to the highway but then he had a problem. It was real steep and rocky to get from the creek bottom up to the road and George was too pooped by then to drag the deer up the cliff. He was thinking of cutting the deer in half when another hunter came along and offered to help George drag the deer the rest of the way up to the road. George got the buck loaded in his car and started back to Phoenix. One happy hunter.

George soon realized that hunting in Arizona was a lot different than hunting in Michigan. More open space and you could see deer a long ways off. A good pair of binoculars or a scope on your rifle was just as important as a compass and a good rifle. So George got himself a pair of binoculars. The next year he hunted one weekend with some guys that he worked with, but realized they didn't have any better idea where to hunt than he did. Then he checked out a couple of areas by himself with no luck.

The last day of the season George went back to the same place that he had killed his deer the year before. That year the Fish and Game Department was trying to reduce the deer population so they were allowing hunters to kill any deer on the last weekend in some areas, no special permit needed. George was sitting up on a point overlooking the spot where he had shot his deer the year before when late in the afternoon he saw a doe and a fawn cross over the top of the ridge across the gully from him. They didn't come down the ridge any closer to him so he decided to take a shot anyway. He figured they were to far away for his old 30-40 but it was the last day of the season so what was there to lose? Maybe the sound of the shot would cause them to come on down. George shot and the doe disappeared, he couldn't see where she went. So George climbed down from his perch and crossed over to the other side and started up the ridge toward the spot where he had last seen the deer. He was about three-quarters of the way up the ridge when the doe came out from behind some bushes. There was some thick brush between George and the deer and he was shooting up hill so when George took another shot, he shot over the top of the deer. The doe just stood there looking for her fawn. George knew that as soon as he racked another shell in to the chamber of his gun, the doe would take off. So George just pulled back the hammer on his gun and took careful aim, pulled the trigger and 'click,' the hammer came down on an empty shell casing in the chamber: "BUCK FEVER". He racked in another shell but the doe was out of sight before he could get another shot. The little fawn came out of the brush and walked right past George, but it was so small that George didn't want to shoot it; there wouldn't have been much meat for the table if he had.

The following year, 1961, George hunted in different areas between Phoenix and Prescott with out any luck. The last weekend of the season he found himself southwest of Prescott near Skull Valley. He started out in the morning working his way up a wash when he came face-to-face with a deer coming down the wash. George leaned his rifle against a bush and brought his binoculars up to get a better look at the deer. He could see it was a buck but couldn't tell if it had forked antlers or not. At that time, in Arizona, a legal buck had to have at least one forked antler, no spike horns were allowed. George and the deer stood there studying each other for a few seconds then the deer whirled and went back the way it had come over a ridge. When the deer turned George could see it had a forked antler but he never had a change to get a shot at it before it was out of sight. Later that afternoon George was sitting on top of the ridge when he saw a nice buck coming up the ridge toward him. George waited and waited until the buck got about one hundred yards from him. Then, it turned broadside to him and started past him. George got off a good shot and the buck took off. He checked the area where the deer was, looking for blood but no luck. He tried to track it but the ground was so hard and dry he couldn't find any tracks. He was so sure he had hit that buck but couldn't find any sign of it. To this day he can't believe he missed that deer but he must have.

The following year, 1962, two of George's brother-in-laws, Victor and Herman, wanted to go hunting with George. They had never hunted before so George had to teach them how to hunt deer. I'm not sure how much they were able to learn from George. George took a week off from work and borrowed an old tent and some camping equipment from his father-in-law. They went back up to Skull Valley where George had missed the buck the year before. They set up the tent and made camp and got set for a week of hunting.

Opening morning they started working their way up a wash right by camp. Victor was in the bottom of the wash, George was about half way up one side of the ridge, and Herman was on the top of the ridge. They got about half way up the wash when they heard a shot from further up the wash. A few minutes later

George saw a nice buck coming right down the bottom of the wash toward them. The buck got right below George and stopped and looked up at him. George had a nice broad side shot at him but George had lost sight of Victor and knew that he was down there in the wash close to where the deer was. So George was afraid to shoot. A stray shot or a ricochet bullet might get Victor. He had to let the buck go. After the buck was gone George was able to locate Victor and he would have been clear of any shot that George would have made. Victor was behind some rocks and bushes and never saw the deer. It must have passed within fifty feet of where Victor was. They hunted hard the rest of that day and the next couple of days. They saw some more deer but they were all too far away to tell what they were or to get a shot at any of them. Then one morning they got up and decided to hunt a couple of ridges over from where they had been hunting. They started working their was up a ridge, this time Victor was on top of one ridge, Herman was about half way up the ridge and George was in the bottom of the wash. They had gone a ways up the ridge when George came to another small canyon that branched off from the main canyon across from where Victor and Herman were. George decided to check it out. He was about half way up the canyon when a doe jumped up and went out over the top. George had a doe permit that year and he took a shot at the doe. He missed but he took about five more steps and another deer jumped up and started back down the canyon in the direction George had come from, across from him. He got off a good shot and saw the deer buckle so he knew he had hit it but it kept going around the corner and out of sight. George crossed over and found a trail of blood. He followed the trail of blood around the corner and then came to the end of the blood trail. George hollered over to Victor and Herman and asked them where the deer had gone. They had seen the doe George shot at and missed go over the top of the ridge but neither one of them saw the other deer that George had shot. George stood there at the end of the blood trail looking around for more blood or tracks. Then he happened to look down and there laid his buck about five feet below him. It had gone over a small ledge on the trail and down the side of the mountain. It looked like he had just jumped off the trail. It was a small buck with about a two-inch fork on each side of his antlers. They had a long drag back to camp but there were three of them so they were able to make it with out too much trouble. They packed up the next day and took the deer back to town. It was too warm to try and keep the deer hanging in a tree another day. Then they came back up the following day and set up camp again and hunted the rest of the week with out any luck.

    The last weekend of the season Herman and George decided to give it one more try. They started up towards Payson. About twenty miles south of Payson George saw what looked like a good area on the West Side of the highway. They pulled off onto a side road and went about a mile off the highway. They hunted up the side of a mountain then started back to the car. George dropped down into a small canyon.

When he came to the end of the canyon it narrowed down and there were two big trees blocking the entrance to the canyon. George had to get down on his hands and knees to crawl under them. He noticed a lot of animal droppings on the ground but didn't have any idea what kind of animal had left the droppings. Just beyond the end of the canyon he came to a waterhole and there were a lot more droppings around the waterhole. Then he heard what he thought was a cow running through the brush. Suddenly a big black bear broke out into a clearing, high tailing it out of there. Then George realized what all those droppings he had seen were. They were bear droppings. George is just glad he didn't meet up with that bear when he was crawling around under the trees. George and Herman went on up north of Payson and found another area that looked good. They hunted about an hour that afternoon before it got dark. Slept in the back of the station wagon that night and hunted the next day without any luck. Didn't even see a deer. Herman went back to Germany after that season so that was the only time he got to go hunting.

The next year, 1963 George and Victor went further west, out toward Bagdad, Arizona. They pulled of the main road along the Santa Maria River and went about a mile off the highway up the side of a small mountain. It was late Friday afternoon before they found a camping place and set up camp. They were going to sleep in the station wagon. They started out early the next morning. They hadn't gone to far when Victor said there is a deer over there across the gully under that ledge. George looked and looked but couldn't see anything. It took George about five minutes to find the deer with his binoculars that Victor had seen with his naked eye. When he did find the deer all he could see was part of it head sticking up over the top of a rock. The deer was lying behind a rock with a tall steep cliff behind it. It was too far away to tell if it was a buck or a doe. George decided he would try and work his way around behind it and come up on top of the cliff over the deer. He told Victor where to go so he would have a good shot at the deer when it came out of there. There was only about one way the deer could go to get out of there. George worked his way over to the top of the cliff and when he looked down he could see it was a small buck. The buck took off and George got a couple of shots at it but didn't come close. Victor meanwhile had gone further around the edge of the ridge that George had told him and he didn't see the buck when it came out of its bed. They hunted most of the day without seeing any more deer then it started to rain. They went back to camp and were going to fix something to eat when suddenly they heard a roar that sounded like a train was coming. They looked around and saw a wall of water rolling down a wash across the canyon from them. They had crossed a dry wash on the way in and George knew that water was headed for that wash. They threw everything in the car and got out of there fast. Hoping to make it back out to the highway before that water blocked the road. About fifteen minutes after they got back across that wash the water came roaring down.

They were glad that they got out of there when they did. They camped that night along the highway and the next morning they walked back in to hunt. It had stopped raining and there was still water flowing in the wash but it wasn't too deep now. About noon they were working their way back toward the car and they sat down on top of a ridge to eat a sandwich when suddenly a big buck came out of the gully below them and started up the other side. They both started shooting. George saw his shot hit just in front of the deer and it turned and started back along the ridge broad side to them. They both got off another round and the buck went down. George was sure that Victor was the one who hit it but Victor didn't think so and he wouldn't put his tag on it. He said it was George's deer. They had a long way to drag it back to the car and then they started home. They had gone about five miles when they saw another deer feeding on the side of a hill about one hundred yards off the road. They both got out and George studied it with his binoculars but couldn't tell if it was a buck or a doe until the deer moved up and over the top of the hill. When it went over the top and was sky lighted George could see horns but it was too late then and they couldn't get a shot at it. Another successful season but it would have been better if they could have gotten the second buck.

  The next two years 1964-1965 were dry years for George. That doesn't mean he didn't try. He hunted hard and long just wasn't able to get a deer. He hunted mostly south west of Prescott around Skull Valley and Hillside. Saw some deer and got a better understanding of the lay of the land. But didn't see any bucks. That was about the time another brother-in law, Bob Jordan, started hunting with him. Victor gave up hunting after the 1965 season. I think the only reason he started hunting was because Mary worried about George running around the mountains by himself and she talked Victor into going with him. Now that George had someone else to go hunting with him Victor gave it up. During this time someone broke into the house and stole George's rifle, shotgun, binoculars, camera, TV and some other things so George had to replace his equipment. George replaced his 30-40 Winchester with an old military style, bolt action 7MM Mauser with a scope and a sling. It had a longer range and was more flat shooting than the old 30-40, much more suitable for the open area that George was now hunting in. George also got a tent, Coleman stove and other camping equipment so he could do more camping.

1966, George had just purchased a pickup with a camper shell on it. Mary, Maria and Cyndy decided to go hunting with him. Bob Jordan went with them. They left late Friday afternoon and went to an area southwest of Hillside. They got there well after dark and set up camp on the bank of a dry river that ran through the area. George had hunted in that area the two previous years so he knew were he was going. Early Saturday morning Bob and George went down the river about a half a mile. The girls stayed in camp. George found a place to sit high up on a point looking down into an area where two canyons came together. About mid morning he saw a deer come over the ridge across the canyon from him. It was a long way off and George had plenty of time to look it over with his binoculars as it made it's way down toward the bottom of the canyon. George was able to see horns so just before it got down to the bottom of the ridge he took his first shot and missed. The second shot dropped it right in the bottom of the canyon. Bob and George dragged the deer back to camp. When they came into camp dragging the deer, Maria and Cyndy both came running shouting, "Daddy got a deer, Daddy got a deer!" Then Cyndy got close to the deer and suddenly she turned around and went crying back to her mommy. She didn't like seeing a dead deer. They never went hunting with Daddy again

    The following year, 1967, George and Bob went back to the same area. They went down the river to just about the same spot where George had killed the deer the year before. Bob went up the ridge on one side of the river and George went up the ridge on the other side. They both found a good spot to sit and settled in for the day. After about an hour or two George heard Bob shoot. He looked through his binoculars and could see Bob getting ready to dress out his buck. George waited a little while then crossed over to where Bob was, he got there just as Bob was finishing dressing out the buck. They were getting ready to start dragging when they heard a shot just over the ridge from them. George grabbed his rifle and jumped up on a rock near where they were standing. George had just gotten in position when a herd of deer came over the ridge heading right at them. A nice buck was leading the way. The deer saw George and Bob veered off to the right behind some bushes. George was ready to shoot when they came out from behind the bushes. The first deer came out and it was a doe, another doe followed it then another before the buck came out and George dropped it right in its tracks. The buck had stopped behind the bushes letting the does go first. So they had two buck to drag out of there that day and it took them a long time to get them both back to camp. Another successful season came to an end.

1968, George and Bob Jordan hunted the first two weekends up around Hillside and Skull Valley with out any luck. The last weekend of the season they didn't feel like making the long drive back up to the mountains so they decided to try hunting in the White Tanks Mountains just west of Phoenix. Some one had told George he saw a herd of deer out there when he was working in the area. They drove into the south end of the mountains and saw a herd of deer in a wash as they were driving in. They couldn't tell if there was a buck in the herd or not. They parked at the bottom of a long canyon and worked their way up to the top they saw some nice tracks but no deer. When they came out on top they could see Phoenix down below them. They were right off the end of Indian School Road, which ended at the base of the mountain. They started back down toward the truck. Bob started straight down and George swung out to the right to make a small circle on the way down. George crossed over the top of a small ridge and there about fifty feet in front of him stood a nice buck looking down at Bob. The deer never saw George and George dropped him right where he stood. Bob didn't see the deer and when he saw George bring his rifle up to shoot he thought that George must have been going to shoot a rabbit because he was aiming at something so close. There was a jeep trail about one hundred feet from where the deer dropped so Bob went down and got the truck and brought it up the trail while George was dressing out the deer.

The following year 1969, George and Bob hunted around Hillside and Skull Valley with out any luck. The last day of the season late in the afternoon they were packing up to go home. They happened to look up at the top of the ridge near where they were parked and saw a couple of deer feeding. They got the binoculars out and started watching them. The deer were about 300 yards away or more. George and Bob were sure that the deer were both does, then a third deer suddenly came over the top of the ridge to join them. There was no doubt that it was a buck. Bob was hunting with a 30-30 and knew they were out of his range so George got his 7MM out. George missed judged the distance and how flat shooting his 7MM was. He aimed high and must have shot right over the top of the buck. They went up there and checked but couldn't find any sign that he had hit the deer. After they got back down to the truck George decided to check and see how flat shooting his 7MM was. He took aim at a large rock on top of the ridge near where the buck was standing. Bob watched with the binoculars and George hit that rock dead center. If George had aimed right at the deer instead of aiming high he probably would have hit the deer. Someone told George later that when you are shooting uphill like that you want to aim low because the barrel of the gun is already pointing up and will cause your bullet to go high.

The next year, 1970, George and Bob were hunting near Hillside again. George went down the river to about the same spot he and Bob had both gotten their bucks in 1967. He was sitting on top of a ridge when he heard a couple of shots off to his right. Then a herd of deer came over the ridge and dropped down in a canyon in front of him, a buck was leading the way. George got off one shot as he went by. Then the whole herd of deer went about half way up the ridge on the left side of the canyon and stopped and started milling around. They didn't seem to know where to go. It took George awhile to pick the buck out of the milling herd but he was finally able to spot him and when he got clear of the does George was able to bring him down. Another successful season came to an end. I can take you down that river bottom and stand in one spot and show you where 4 bucks were killed.

In the early 1970's the Arizona Game and Fish Department decided that too many hunters were concentrating in the areas close to the bigger cities and town and not enough hunters were going to some of the more remote areas of the state. So they decided to go to a permit-only hunting season. They divided the state into about fifty units and would issue a certain number of permits in each unit, depending on the deer count. Every one would have to apply for a permit and take their chances in a drawing. You could submit your application with three choices. If you didn't get drawn for your first choice your permit would go into the area of your second choice, if that unit was full then it would go to your third choice. There were some units that always had permits left over after the drawing and some times you could get a permit for one of those units just by applying for it and some times they would hold a second drawing just before deer season for the remaining permits.

George wasn't very lucky in the drawing. He never got back to his favorite area around Hillside where he killed most of his deer. George and Bob Jordan hunted around Skull Valley a couple of years without any luck and a couple of years they hunted just west of Phoenix and south of Wickenburg. There wasn't much in that area but it was close to home and they didn't have far to drive but no deer. In 1977 or 1978 they hunted just north of Crown King. Bob wounded a buck on Saturday morning and they tracked it for over 2 hours before they were able to get it. George didn't hunt any more that year.

1979 George's son-in-law, Robert, started hunting with him. They got permits for the area south of Prescott and north of Crown King. They scouted the area before deer season and settled on an area around Battle Flats. They hunted there opening weekend and saw a lot of deer but no bucks. On the way home the road ran along side of Turkey Creek and George saw some ears sticking up above the creek bank when they came around a curve. He stopped and there was a herd of deer down there in the creek bottom. One of them was a buck. Robert jumped out of the truck and tried to get his rifle out from under the seat. The buck was only about thirty feet away and Robert had a loaded pistol strapped on his hip, the buck was close enough for him to shoot with his pistol but he wanted to get his rifle. The buck just walked away while Robert was trying to get his rifle and by the time he did get his rifle out and loaded the buck was gone. George just sat there and laughed. I think the buck was laughing at Robert too. [2]

After hunting season was over in Arizona George took a couple of weeks off work and went back to Michigan to hunt for the first time in thirty years. He had forgotten what it was like to hunt in Michigan compared to Arizona. For one thing Michigan had snow, tracking snow. You could tell where the deer had been and see where they were going. But the snow was cold and wet. Your feet got cold standing around and the snow dropped down the back of your neck when you walked under a tree. You needed 3 or 4 pair of gloves to keep your hands warm and dry. It didn't warm up during the day. In Arizona, you could start out in the morning with the temperature around freezing and by mid-afternoon be hunting in your shirtsleeves with the temperature in the mid-fifties or sixties. George didn't get a deer and if he had seen a buck he probably would

---

[2] Editor's Note: It should be pointed out that there is a reason that soldiers go to basic training and advanced infantry training *before* going into battle and that novice deer hunters are afforded no such luxury...

have been shivering too much to hit it. George was glad to get back to Arizona to get thawed out.

The summer of 1980 George got a 4-wheel drive Scout. Now they could get back off the beaten track into some of the more remote places that they couldn't get to with a regular

The Scout near Tres Amigos

truck. George and Robert hunted around Battle Flats, the same area they hunted the year before. They saw a lot of deer but didn't get a shot at any of them. One morning George was working his way along the side of a ridge when he heard something in the bushes. The bushes were real small. Only about two or three feet high so he didn't think it was a deer. George just stood there waiting and suddenly a javelina came out of the brush, then another, and another. There were twelve to fifteen javelinas in that herd and they were all around George. In front of him, behind him, one came to within five or six feet of George. The javelinas were just feeding and didn't pay any attention to George until he moved and then they all took off in a hurry. One night after supper George and Robert were sitting around the campfire and suddenly there was an explosion. At first they couldn't figure out what had happened. Then Robert realized that he had put a bullet into his shirt pocket and it must have fallen out into the fire when he bent over to put some wood on the fire. It blew a hole in the fender of the Scout but thank goodness no one was hurt and nothing was seriously damaged.[3]

1981 and 1982, Bob Jordan and his son Bobby joined George and Robert and they hunted in the same area around Battle Flats. Bob got a shot at a buck but missed but no one got a deer even though they saw a lot of deer. That was the last year that Bob Jordan hunted with George.

1983, they were not very lucky in the draw. No one got drawn for a permit. When it came time to summit an application for the second drawing George was in Michigan. Robert put in an application for an area close to town between Cave Creek and Bartlett Lake. He was lucky enough to get a permit. So when deer season opened George went with Robert even though he didn't have a permit and couldn't hunt. They found a jeep trail that ran along the top of a ridge with steep canyons on both sides just west of Bartlett Lake. They followed it back until it ended at a small mountain

---

[3] Editor's Note: There may be some dispute on the damaged caused by the exploding bullet...there were no ballistics tests run.

peak. They hunted around there most of the day then late in the afternoon drove down off the side of the mountain and found a flat level place to camp. They unloaded the Scout and set up camp then they walked over to the edge of one of the steep canyons and sat there glassing the canyon below them until it started getting dark. They went back to the camp and George walked over to take a look into another one of the side canyons. He was about twenty-five yards from camp when he walked up to the edge of the canyon and looked over. Just then a nice buck got up from his bed on the other side of the canyon. George dropped down so the buck couldn't see him and started waving at Robert. Robert just stood there looking at George and wondering what is that crazy guy doing. George didn't want to yell or he would scare the buck so he put both hands up beside his head and spread his fingers to simulate a set of horns. Robert got the message and grabbed his rifle and came running. George told him where he had seen the buck and when Robert looked over the side of the canyon the buck was still standing there under a tree right were George had first seen it. Robert dropped it right in its bed with one shot. It was getting late and they went back to camp to get a couple of flashlight and had to dress the deer out using the flashlights to see. Then they had to drag the buck back to camp in the dark. It was a good thing that had the flashlights with them because they sure needed them that night. It was Robert's first deer. They hung the buck up on the side of the truck and spent the night there and went home the following morning.

1984 George and Robert got permits for the same area between Cave Creek and Bartlett Lake. They found a nice camping spot and set up camp. The first day they didn't see any deer. The morning of the second day they had gone about a half-mile from camp when Robert had to answer Mother Nature's call. He went behind some bushes and George sat there glassing the area. George was glassing the ridge across the canyon from them when he spotted a herd of deer. George was able to pick a buck out of the herd and even though they were a long way off he decided to take a shot. When George shot, Robert came charging out of the bushes with his pants down around his knees and his rifle in his hand looking for something to shoot at.[4] George missed and the deer went over the top of the ridge. George wasn't sure if he had missed or not so he dropped down into the canyon and up the other side. When he got to the top of the ridge the deer were still milling around on the other side of the ridge. They took off and George and Robert both got a couple of shots at them but both missed. That was the only deer they saw that year.

    The summer of 1985, George and Mary purchased a house in Yarnell. Now they could use it as a base camp for hunting and not have to set up a tent and camp out all the time. George still enjoyed camping out but Robert preferred to be able to come in and take a shower and sleep in a warm bed rather than crawl into a sleeping bag at the end of the day.

---

[4] Editor's Note: It should be noted that the relief of oneself in the wilds, while entirely necessary, brings with it a certain amount of unknown danger...

They were able to get permits for an area north of Yarnell and south of Prescott about fifteen miles north of Yarnell. George and Robert scouted the area before deer season and settled on an area along the headwaters of the Hassayampa River. The first day they saw a few deer but no bucks. Robert was setting on top of a small mountain peak when a couple of F-4 Jets from Luke Airforce Base flew right over him. They were so low that Robert said he could feel the heat from the engine of the jet that flew over him and the other one was off to the side and he could see the pilot in that one. Sunday morning as they were driving in to start hunting, they saw a buck coming down a draw towards the road. George stopped and Robert grabbed his rifle and jumped out of the Scout and started shooting. Robert hit the buck four times before it went down, but he got it.[5] That was the end of their hunting for that day. The next weekend George hunted by himself. He was working his way up a ridge and it started to rain. He had a poncho in his backpack so he put it on but the rain didn't let up. He was thinking of calling it quits and heading back to the car when he jumped a deer. As it went over the top of the ridge he could see it was a buck. He followed it over the ridge and glassed the area in front of him and spotted the buck lying under a tree on the next ridge. It was raining real hard now and George could hardly see through his scope but he got off one shot but missed. Then he called it a day.

---

[5] Editor's Note: The editor still believes that the deer was wearing kevlar or some other bullet-resistant material contrary to the laws of nature…

1986, George and Robert got drawn for an area west of Wickenburg and south of Congress. It was only about twenty-five miles from Yarnell so they could stay in Yarnell and drive down there to hunt. They saw a few deer but no bucks; it wasn't a very good area. One day George was headed back towards the truck when he walked through a patch of jumping cactus. One of the cactus balls jumped off the bush and got him on the hand. He tried to knock it off but couldn't. He tried to pry it off with his knife but it just rolled around and jumped back on to another part of his hand. He finally had to put it down on the ground and step on it to get it off his hand. He still had a lot of cactus spines in his hand and had to use a pair of pliers to pull them all out when he got back to the truck. It sure hurt.[6]

George retired in the summer of 1987 now he could hunt the entire season not just on weekends. George and Robert got drawn for the area North of Yarnell where they hunted in 1985. George went up to Yarnell and stayed at the house the full season. Robert came up and hunted with him on the weekends. George hunted long and hard that year and saw a lot of deer but no bucks. He didn't get a shot all season.

1988, George and Robert got drawn for the same area. George only hunted for about five days because his father was dying of cancer and he cut off his hunting early and went back to Michigan to be with his father who passed

---

[6] Editor's Note: The editor was impressed with George's courage. He did not cry or scream as this Stephen King novel unfolded before his eyes.

away on December 8, 1988. George didn't see any bucks that year. He hunted a few days in Michigan while he was there, without any luck.

1989 THE SHOT

1989, George and Robert got drawn for an area northwest of Wickenburg. They scouted the area before deer season and settled on an area near the Santa Maria River and the Joshua Forest. It was about thirty-five miles from Yarnell so they decided to camp out rather that drive back and forth from Yarnell. George went up there on Thursday and set up camp and hunted all day Friday and only saw one doe. Robert was supposed to come up Friday night after work and join him. Robert got lost on the way in and made a wrong turn and ended up sleeping in his truck that night.[7] He didn't find the camp until Saturday afternoon. George didn't see any deer on Saturday. Sunday morning they saw a herd of deer and there was one buck with them. Robert got a shot at him but missed. Monday they saw no deer but on Tuesday they saw the same herd they saw on Sunday but they were not able to get a shot at the buck. They didn't hunt too much on Wednesday and drove up to Yarnell to take a shower and rest up. Thursday morning when they came back from Yarnell they decided to hunt across the canyon from where they had seen the deer on Sunday and Tuesday. They drove down a jeep trail on top of the ridge until the road came to an end. They parked the Scout and Robert went left and George went right.

---

[7] Editor's Note: "Lost" is such an ugly word...

Suddenly Robert came running over to where George was and said the herd of deer was coming down the bottom of the canyon right below them. The deer came down to a small water hole in the canyon and stopped for a drink. Then the does started up the other side of the canyon. They were a long way off but there was a white rock cliff just above the water hole and after the does left they were able to see horns on the deer that stayed behind. George wasn't sure he wanted to shoot a deer down in the bottom of that canyon and have to drag it all the

The Shot

way up. But Robert took a shot so George took a shot too. The buck had just started up the other side when George shot and he saw his bullet hit just below the buck. The buck stopped and looked around trying to figure out where the shots were coming from. George got the buck in his cross hairs and aimed high for his second shot. The buck dropped right in his tracks. It took George twenty minutes to get down the canyon to where the deer was and after he cleaned him out it took George and Robert over two hours to drag him back up to the Scout. The buck went down at 8:45AM and it was 12:30PM before they got it back to the Scout. It is a good thing it was a small buck. They went back to the area later with a range finder and estimated that the shot was over three hundred yards and George had hit the buck in the head just behind the ear. That is why Robert refers to it as THE SHOT. That would also be the last deer that George would shoot.

The following is Robert's version of what happened that day.

THE SHOT
By Robert B. Curtis.

The day was warm; the sun shining over the rugged hills as the sound of distant jets could be heard piercing the silence. George was glassing a stand of white rock some two hundred yards down in the distance. For four days he and Bob had stalked a sizable herd of mule deer. It was an ironic treasure, eight deer including a young buck in an area where the very cut of the land and sparseness of foliage spoke of great desert and barrenness beyond all reason. The scouting of some months before and the sheer size of the unit had left mild, resigned pall hanging over the hunt. But they had found the herd. A magnificent herd under any circumstances and they had seen and shot at the young buck earlier in the week.

Patience was their watchword. They had learned, over what seemed like a thousand hunts, that the muley was a creature of habit. And on that earlier day they had followed the herd down into the bottom of the strange white rock ravine and had found water: cool, clear water gushing up from a hidden spring. They knew that those deer would be back.

The two of them were weary. Up early after a restless night of sleep in the comfort of the Yarnell house they fought against the feeling of impending failure that had followed them on their hunting trips since the last kill four years earlier and the one two years before that. Here it was only four days left in the hunt and the morning feeding period was in full swing. George was an immensely patient glasser and Bob was not. Bob had secreted a book with him onto the rock where he sat reading taking only an occasional sweep of the surrounding terrain with his binoculars. This morning as he looked up from his book, his eye caught movement in the south end of the ravine and he picked up his glasses to take what he thought was another boring glance. He was certain that the deer had already left the area for their alternate feeding ground and as he glassed down into the ravine against the white rock he spotted them. A fawn and then a doe and a moment later the buck stepped out into the open! He was startled momentarily and rose quickly to retrieve his rifle. Suddenly he felt excited that a buck was down in the bottom and had not detected them and he remembered that George had not taken one in over nineteen years. Bob trotted down the jeep trail toward where George was glassing as he began loading the magazine of his rifle and the frenzied look he wore gave George a good idea that his son-in-law must have spotted something.

"J' ya see' em?" George asked in his typically calm. Midwestern manner.

"Down in the bottom!" Bob gasp as he pointed and raised his binoculars to look.

Their position was perfect, high atop the ravine the deer could not see, hear nor detect their scent. George glassed the ravine and finally spotted them also.

"Is the buck with them?" He asked as he searched the surrounding bushes.

Bob had already laid down on the ground and had placed his rifle over a large flat rock for extra support. He took aim down into the ravine to see if he could spot his target against the bright white background.

"I saw him real clear," Bob replied excitedly, "He's right there and I'm shooting!"

Bob had spent years carefully conditioning himself against the indignity of "Buck Fever" vowing never again to let the presence of a buck fluster him. But it had all gone out the window at that moment. George sat down quietly on rock next to Bob and also aimed his rifle.

"Where's he at?" George asked, the barest hint of adrenaline beginning to make its was to the surface.

"I'm gonna take a shot!" was Bob's only hyperventilated reply.

A resounding CRACK split the air as Bob's .243 caliber rifle spit a small amount of fire and through the scope he could see that he had missed badly. Suddenly, a loud roar next to him silenced even the thunder of the fighter jets that had come out to play at war in the sky above them, spewing fire from the formidable 7mm rifle that George always carried. And through his scope Bob could see dirt kick up down in the bottom of the ravine just inches from the buck as it turned confusedly and started up the side toward safety with the rest of the herd. Bob fired again and missed, the small size of his own weapon failing him. But as he continued watching through his scope and George again fired, he could see the buck suddenly stagger heavily and then fall in a heap on the side of the small hill just up from the bottom of the ravine. The entire herd, minus one, was now gone.

Bob instantly leaped into the air. "You got ' em!" he shouted springing like a young buck himself over the rock. "What a shot, you got 'em!"

Bob clapped George on the shoulder enthusiastically as if he had just scored the winning touchdown and George simply responded by trying to look around him to take account and insure himself of his kill. Bob stopped as if momentarily stunned, suddenly realizing the nature of the shot and as he turned and stared down into the ravine without binoculars or rifle scope and his eyes went wide. The fallen deer was a mere speck on the open hillside, its natural camouflage making it nearly impossible to spot. It was an incredible shot, a world class shot! The kind of shot that people only read about in magazines, But George had *done it and it was to become the stuff of legend, putting himself alongside the likes of Daniel Boone, Davy Crockett and Sergeant York. And all that from an ex-sailor with a tiny, barely functioning 4X rifle scope!*

The two men stood on the edge of the steep ravine looking down at the fallen deer. Their first rational thought after the thrill of the kill was the utter madness of their action. It was easily two hundred yards straight down to the deer itself and who could tell how far down the side of the ravine. They judged the angle of descent at about sixty degrees, which meant the angle of ascent dragging a deer, would be more like ninety! But it was their first deer in over four years and it was still only eight-forty in the morning. They told themselves that they not only had the rest of the day to drag the deer out but the rest of the week! As George started down the side of the ravine, Bob figured silently that it would probably take all four remaining days to bring the animal home.

It took George a full twenty minutes to climb down to his fallen quarry and he immediately began the task of cleaning out the innards of the animal. The size of the deer was average and the rack was small and unusual. It carried a small point and spur on one side and a strange, downwardly curved antler on the other. George had taken many deer before, all larger than this one, but after nineteen years this was the best thing that ever happened to him. At least that day.

Bob ran back up to move the truck closer to where they would attempt to drag out the deer and it took him a good forty minutes to make his way down into the ravine and up the other side. When he arrived, George was putting the finishing touches on what looked like a scene from the horror film, TEXAS CHAINSAW MASSACRE, deer innards piled neatly and blood spilt everywhere. George was there with his pocketknife, blood completely covering his forearms. All he lacked was the deep demonic grin of Leatherface, Freddy Krueger or any of the other cinema killers. But to George this was as natural as breathing the fresh air or drinking the icy cold water from the spring below.

As George completed his task and washed up, two of the practicing fighters jets flew closely overhead, hugging the dangerous terrain as if to pay tribute to a successful campaign.

For a brief moment, as the two men prepared the deer for dragging, a slight feeling of anticlimax permeated the morning air, but what followed over the next two hours was more on the scale of Mallory's historical ascent of the north face of Everest. The deer seemed to weigh easily two hundred pounds as the two men dragged it at an ever-increasing angle. Step by step, inch by inch, over rock and cactus and bush without solid footing they willed that animal toward the top. And each time they looked up, the summit seemed to grow further away from them as if the land were refusing to give up its dead

But slowly they continued, stopping to drop heavily amid the rocks; sweat and thirst threatening to consume them at every mo-

ment. But finally, after a trek that made the infamous Bataan Death March look like a boy scout hike the two men dragged the deer the last three feet to the open back end of the truck and collapsed against its sides struggling to catch their breath. The greatest feats in sports were no match for their accomplishment, as Bob thought, "intense human drama, the thrill of victory," and looking down at his own tired boots, " the agony of defeat."

Finally, the two men loaded the deer into the back of the truck and stepped once more to gaze down upon the magnificent scene, the distance having grown even more dizzying in their weariness. Both gazed silently out toward the spot where the deer had fallen.

After a minute or two, Bob turned toward George and smiled.

"World class shot," he said, "World class shot."

George simply nodded. A world class shot it had been and now only the story was left to tell.

In 1990 George traded his Scout in for a 1986 Dodge Power Ram with 4-wheel drive. That year he got drawn for an area west of Wickenburg where he had hunted in 1986. It was not a very good area and he didn't even see a deer.

In 1991 they were lucky enough to get drawn for the area north of Yarnell where they had hunted in 1987 and 1988. Wayne came out from Michigan to hunt with them. He couldn't get a permit so he just tagged along and got to see a lot of country that he had never seen before. George and Wayne took the tent and set up camp down in the flats along the headwaters of the Hassayampa River. Robert and his son, Bobby, came up and hunted with them the first weekend. They camped out for about a week and then broke camp and drove back and forth from Yarnell for the last week. They saw a lot of deer but no bucks until the last weekend of the season. That morning on the way in to hunt they dropped Wayne off at the foot of a small mountain then they drove up to the top of the mountain. George and Robert found a place to set and Wayne worked his way up to them. Wayne jumped two nice bucks and they came right up the mountain to where George had left Robert sitting. The only problem was that Robert had moved around to the side to get out of the wind and didn't see the deer. According to Wayne the bucks went right by close to where Robert was suppose to be.[8]

After the deer season was over in Arizona George went back to Michigan with Wayne. They had always wanted to go deer hunting in the Upper Peninsula of Michigan so Wayne got a camp trailer and they went up there. A friend of Wayne's had some property up there and he let them hunt on his land. The first day they were there, before deer season opened, they were sitting in the trailer and a doe came out of the woods and walked by within twenty-five feet of the trailer. They had a lot of snow and saw a lot of deer but no bucks.

---

[8] Editor's Note: Extra-sensory Perception is not one of Robert's strong points...

They stayed there a week then a big snowstorm came in and they headed home.

In 1992 George was not very lucky in the draw. They didn't get a permit in the first drawing so they put in for a second drawing and got a permit for an area south of Buckeye and north of Gila Bend. George and Robert went down there scouting a week before season opened. It was God forsaken country and about the only wildlife in the area were gila monsters and scorpions. It was so hot and dry that they saw a coyote chasing a jackrabbit and they were both walking. They didn't see any deer signs at all so when deer season opened they didn't even bother to go hunting.

1993, they were back in the area north of Yarnell. The first weekend of season as they were on the way home late in the afternoon they saw a couple of deer feeding, one was a buck. George got off a couple of shots but missed. The next morning they went back to the same area. They parked the truck and Robert went to the right and George went to the left around a small hill. George hadn't gone to far when a buck got up about fifty yards in front of him. It was standing there broadside to him. George took careful aim and pulled the trigger and nothing happened. He checked his safety and tried again and couldn't pull the trigger. Then he noticed that the bolt on his rifle had jiggled open and was acting like a second safety. He closed the bolt but by then the buck had taken off and he was only able to get a couple of wild shots as the buck went over the top of the ridge. Robert saw the deer come over the top of the ridge but wasn't able to get a shot at at it. They saw a lot more deer that year but no more bucks.

1994, 1995, and 1996 they were lucky enough to get drawn for the same area north of Yarnell. They saw a lot of deer but no bucks at least not any that were close enough for them to see any horns on. George had twisted his knee a couple of years before when he was hunting and now that he was getting older it was starting to bother him. It would be especially bad early in the morning and when the weather got cold and damp. So he was starting to slow down a lot and was not able to cover as much territory as he did before. The terrain was also starting to change. What were once small ridges and mountain ranges now loomed as insurmountable mountain peaks. Small gullies and washes now appeared as steep inaccessible canyons. The older you get the higher and steeper those mountains get and they are much harder to climb. So George didn't hunt as much or as hard as he use to.

In 1997 they got drawn for an area just south of where they had been hunting the years before. It was closer to Yarnell and included the town of Yarnell so George could have shot a deer in his own back yard if one had come along. When deer season arrived George wasn't sure if he would go hunting or not. Mary had just gotten out of the hospital and she needed someone to be with her 24/7. Maria said she could stay with her over the weekend so George, Robert and Bobby could go hunting. They went up to Yarnell Friday night and hunted Saturday and part of Sunday around Peeples Valley. Robert saw a couple of deer but

George didn't see any. That was the last time George went hunting. Mary's health became a problem and George had to take care of her until she passed away in 2001. After that George just didn't have the desire to go hunting again. I guess he was just getting old. But he had a lot of memories of his earlier hunting days to fall back on. Some were good and some not so good. Some hits and a lot of misses. But they were all good times to remember. On George and Mary's fortieth wedding anniversary their grandson, Bobby, gave George a T-shirt that said " MY WIFES GOING TO LEAVE ME IF I GO HUNTING ONE MORE TIME. I'M SURE GOING TO MISS HER." Now George misses them both, Mary and his hunting.

    I want to close this with a little story that has nothing to do with deer hunting but is a hunting story nonetheless and goes back to the earlier days in Arizona. One day George and a friend were hunting doves and rabbits by Skunk Creek near Bell Road and Fifty-ninth Avenue. That was before the area was developed and there were no houses there. They saw a rabbit go into a pile of brush so George got up on top of the brush pile and started jumping up and down to scare the rabbit out. He was standing on a small branch about three or four inches in diameter. He thought it was strange that when he stopped jumping the bushes kept on rattling. He looked around and then just jiggled the branch he was standing on a couple of times. He heard the rattling again and now was able to see where it was coming from. About three feet in front of him down under the bushes was a diamondback rattlesnake all coiled and ready to strike. George just lowered his shotgun and blasted away. The snake was about five feet long but I don't think it could have gotten George with all the brush that was between them. That was the only close encounter George had with a rattlesnake in all the years he hunted in Arizona. Don't know what happened to the rabbit and they say rattlesnakes travel in pairs so they didn't hang around to find out if it was true or not.

Epilogue

Nowadays you can expect to find George at the senior center doing his aerobics, hanging out with the girls, or eating lunch three or four days a week. When he is not at the center he is home playing cribbage or solitaire on the computer or writing. He has been writing some short stories as well as working on this autobiography.

George Finally Finished

Which he has just finished.